CONTENTS

MAKE THAT GRADE MANAGEMENT

THIRD EDITION

Margaret Linehan

GILL & MACMILLAN

Gill & Macmillan Ltd
Hume Avenue
Park West
Dublin 12
with associated companies throughout the world
www.gillmacmillan.ie

978 0 7171 4985 8

Print origination by O'K Graphic Design, Dublin
Printed by GraphyCems, Spain

The paper used in this book comes from the wood pulp of managed forests. For every tree felled, at least one tree is planted, thereby renewing natural resources.

TABLES

FIGURES

1
INTRODUCTION TO MANAGEMENT

Objectives

This chapter will help you to:
- define management
- trace the historical development of management
- identify the main contributors to management theory
- understand the similarities and differences between various management perspectives.

1.1 Management defined

This chapter begins with an examination of what is meant by **management**. While there are many definitions of management, there is no universal agreement on what is meant by the term. From as early as 1903 management has been defined in various ways, for example, Taylor (1911):

> Knowing exactly what you want people to do, and then seeing that they do it in the best and cheapest way.

Taylor's definition, however, is rather simplistic, as management is a much more complex process. In 1916, Henri Fayol stated that:

> To manage is to forecast and plan, to organise, to command, to co-ordinate and to control.

Fayol's definition of management therefore gives us six key elements:
- forecasting
- planning
- organising
- commanding
- co-ordinating
- controlling.

Fayol believed that *forecasting* and *planning* were concerned with looking at future activities in an organisation and drawing up plans of action to deal with situations which may arise. He viewed *organising* in terms of having the people and resources necessary to carry out organisational planning in a logical manner. He described *commanding* as 'maintaining activity among the personnel', that is, having a manager with a plan for a group of activities that have the same objective. Similarly, he viewed *co-ordinating* as a unifying activity, facilitating managers and employees to work together to achieve organisational goals. Finally, *controlling* meant that activities happened in accordance with the established policies and practices of an organisation. Most of these activities are very task oriented, rather than people oriented.

Fayol's perspective viewed organisations from the top downwards, emphasising the hierarchical aspects of organisations. His definition has been criticised in the context of the flatter structures of modern organisations and of increased employee participation in decision-making processes.

Recent management theorists offer different definitions of management, such as Griffin (2008):

> Management is a set of activities (including planning and decision-making, organising, leading, and controlling) directed at an organisation's resources (human, financial, physical, and information) with the aim of achieving organisational goals in an efficient and effective manner.

It can be seen from Griffin's definition that the activities suggested by Fayol for understanding management are still incorporated into modern-day management theories. It is important, however, to note that Griffin's definition highlights *the achieving of organisational goals in an efficient and effective manner*. **Efficient** means using resources wisely and in a cost-effective way. Griffin defines **effective** as making the right decisions and successfully implementing them.

Similarly, Naylor (2004) stated that:

> Management is the process of achieving organisational objectives, within a changing environment, by balancing efficiency, effectiveness and equity, obtaining the most from limited resources, and working with and through people.

Naylor's definition consists of five key terms:

1. **Achieving organisational objectives** — setting realistic targets or objectives and achieving them successfully.

2. **Within a changing environment** — organisations operate in a dynamic environment. The environment consists of two major forces, namely, the

macro environment and the micro environment (see Chapter 2). *Macro-environmental factors* include:

- the economic environment
- technology
- the political and legal environment
- the social or cultural environment
- the international environment.

Micro-environmental factors consist of:

- employees
- investors
- competitors
- suppliers
- distributors
- customers.

3. **Balancing efficiency, effectiveness and equity** — combining the changing of inputs into outputs and achieving desired results while at the same time being fair to all employees.

4. **Obtaining the most from limited resources** — managers need to understand that they do not have unlimited resources and must therefore use the resources available to them as efficiently as possible.

5. **With and through other people** — having the right people at the right place at the right time to achieve organisational objectives.

1.2 Managing at different levels of the organisation

Organisations generally have three levels of management, represented by top managers, middle managers and first-line managers.

Top managers make up the relatively small group of executives who manage the overall organisation. Titles found in this group include president, vice-president and chief executive officer (CEO). Top managers create the organisation's goals, overall strategy and operating policies.

Middle managers are primarily responsible for implementing the policies and plans developed by top managers and for supervising and co-ordinating the activities of lower level managers.

First-line managers supervise and co-ordinate the activities of operating employees. First-line managers typically spend a large proportion of their time supervising the work of subordinates.

Managerial Roles

Henry Mintzberg (a Canadian academic) closely observed the day-to-day activities of a group of CEOs by literally following them around and taking notes on what they did. From his observations, Mintzberg concluded that managers play ten different roles, as summarised in Table 1.1, and that these roles fall into three basic categories: interpersonal, informational and decisional.

Category	*Role*	*Sample Activities*
INTERPERSONAL	Figurehead	Attending ribbon-cutting ceremony for new plant.
	Leader	Encouraging employees to improve productivity.
	Liaison	Co-ordinating activities of two project groups.
INFORMATIONAL	Monitor	reports to stay abreast of developments.
	Disseminator	Sending e-mails outlining new organisational initiatives.
	Spokesperson	Making a speech to discuss growth plans.
	Scanning industry	
DECISIONAL	Entrepreneur	Developing new ideas for innovation.
	Disturbance handler	Resolving conflict between two subordinates.
	Resource allocator	Reviewing and revising budget requests.
	Negotiator	Reaching agreement with unions.

Table 1.1 Ten basic managerial roles

1.3 Management theories

The **classical management** perspective emerged during the late 1890s and early 1900s and consisted of two distinct areas:

- *Scientific management* was concerned with the individual worker and issues such as the division of work, the establishment of authority and developing solutions to problems of labour inefficiency.

- *Classical organisation* theory, on the other hand, focused on managing the total organisation.

Early management theorists included: Frederick Winslow Taylor in the United States, Henri Fayol in France and Max Weber in Germany.

Frederick Winslow Taylor

F.W. Taylor (1856–1915) is considered to be a pioneer in the scientific management field and he is often referred to as 'the father of scientific management'. His theories were based on his experience as a shop-floor worker and later as a manager.

OBSERVATIONS	Making detailed timings with stopwatches enabled Taylor to analyse each aspect of the production process.
EXPERIMENTS	Taylor developed a science of work and devised experiments in order to achieve maximum efficiency.
STANDARDISATION	From the data collected from observations and experiments, instructions were published which were to be followed by workers. Standardisation implied that managers had to ensure that workers were provided with the proper equipment and that this was used effectively.
SELECTION AND TRAINING	Taylor showed that output could be increased with employees feeling less tired and earning up to 60% more pay as a result of the correct selection and training of personnel and the matching of staff to tasks.
PAYMENT BY RESULTS	Taylor believed that workers were primarily motivated by pay. He experimented with differential piece-work plans which he believed would lead to increased prosperity for all. Piece-work systems were at the centre of scientific management.
CO-OPERATION	Management and workers were required to co-operate if everyone was to benefit from scientific management. Taylor, however, believed that the workers should remain under the control of their management and accept that management would be responsible for determining what was to be done and how the work was to be done.

Table 1.2 Taylor's principles of scientific management

At the beginning of the twentieth century many industrial plants were mechanised, yet the plants still employed thousands of staff to feed and unload the machines and materials. Business was expanding and capital was readily available, but labour was in short supply. The problem for management, therefore, was to organise the existing labour more efficiently. According to Wallace *et al.* (2004), this situation led to the emergence of modern management as a result of the need to plan, control, direct and organise the use of equipment, capital, materials and people in the factories. During this time, working conditions were poor and workers could do little about this as they had little or no economic or political power.

Taylor observed that few, if any, workers put more than minimal effort into their daily work. He called this lack of effort *soldiering*, which he subdivided into *natural soldiering*, that is, workers' natural tendency to spare effort, and *systematic soldiering*, that is, the deliberate and organised restriction of work rate by employees. Taylor believed that soldiering was primarily a result of fear of unemployment. It was against this background that Taylor developed his ideas on management.

Taylor was primarily interested in the efficiency of working methods, and the solutions he devised were based on his own experience at work. He analysed each job by breaking it down into its component parts and then designed the quickest and best methods of operation for each part. Scientific management or 'Taylorism' derived from six basic activities, as shown in Table 1.2.

Scientific management improved productivity in an era of mass production, but the emphasis was on quantity rather than on quality of production. Scientific management also identified work design, rewards, employee development and co-operation — all still important in modern organisations. Aspects of Taylorism are still visible in some manufacturing organisations today, for example, a specialised machinist operating one machine at one particular work station.

One of the main disadvantages of scientific management was that it failed to take the human or social context of workers into account. Instead, Taylorist managers believed that pay was the most important reward for employees and, accordingly, assumed that the more workers earned the happier they would be. Scientific management also took the thinking out of work for the workers and treated them as another tool in the organisation or as automatons. Scientific management theorists, however, did not sufficiently take into account the actual needs of workers in relation to matters such as working conditions, job satisfaction and having a say in matters which directly affected them.

Other contributors to scientific management who extended Taylor's work included, for example, Henry Gantt (1861–1919), and a husband and wife team, Frank Gilbreth (1868–1924) and Lillian Gilbreth (1878–1972). These theorists made significant contributions to the study of work.

Henry Gantt was an American mechanical engineer and management consultant. Gantt's main contribution to management theory was the Gantt chart, where a worker's progress was recorded. There are many variations of the Gantt chart; an example is given in Figure 1.1. The chart was originally set up to indicate graphically the extent to which a worker had or had not achieved his or her assigned tasks. Modern project management software still includes this critical function. The chart was divided horizontally into hours, days or weeks, with the task indicated by a straight line across the appropriate time span. The amount of the task achieved was shown by another straight line parallel to the original.

The Gantt chart is still accepted as an important management tool today, it provides a graphic schedule for the planning and controlling of work, and records progress towards stages of a project. The chart has a modern variation, Program Evaluation and Review Technique (PERT).

Period	Day 1	Day 1	Day 1	Day 1	Day 1
Planned output	200 units	200 units	200 units	200 units	200 units
Actual output	150 units	170 units	180 units	200 units	210 units
Daily actual					
Cumulative					

Figure 1.1 Gantt chart

Gantt also introduced a payment system where performance below what was planned on the worker's chart still qualified the worker for the day-rate, but achievement of the actual planned work earned the worker a large bonus. From this payment system, Gantt discovered that if one worker realised that the task could be achieved, many other workers quickly accomplished similar achievements, which resulted in workers learning for themselves and making greater use of their time. Gantt also believed that there was not just 'one best way' of completing a task, but a way 'which seems to be the best at the moment'.

The husband and wife team of Frank and Lillian Gilbreth used scientific management principles to eliminate unnecessary movements for bricklayers. The Gilbreths observed, for example, that as a direct result of analysing and redesigning the work methods of some bricklayers, the number of movements in laying bricks was reduced from eighteen to five per brick. The

Gilbreths' focus was less on time than on the elimination of unnecessary movements, which became known as 'motion study'.

Although the work of the Gilbreths is often associated with that of Frederick Winslow Taylor, there was a substantial philosophical difference between the Gilbreths and Taylor. The symbol of Taylorism was the stopwatch; Taylor was primarily concerned with reducing process times. The Gilbreths, on the other hand, sought to make processes more efficient by reducing the motions involved. They saw their approach as more concerned with workers' welfare than Taylorism, which workers themselves often perceived as primarily concerned with profit.

Henri Fayol

Henri Fayol (1841–1925) was a French mining engineer who believed that his fourteen principles of management were applicable to any organisation and were capable of adaptation according to need. He observed that these principles were the ones that he had to apply most frequently during his career. Table 1.3 shows the principles listed in the order set out by Fayol.

It is important to recognise that Fayol's principles were written in a different era and have been criticised for being incapable of meeting the demands of dynamic modern organisations. For example, Fayol's principles of management take a perspective which looks at organisations from the top downwards, emphasising the hierarchical aspects of organisations.

A primary difference, therefore, between Fayol and Taylor was that Taylor viewed management processes from the bottom up, while Fayol viewed it from the top down.

Fayol was the first theorist to devise a set of management principles which could be passed on to others. Fayol's principles, therefore, had more widespread applications for organisations than Taylor's scientific management, which was largely centred on the shop floor.

1	**DIVISION OF WORK**	Increases productivity work using the same effort.
2	**AUTHORITY**	The right to give orders and have the orders followed.
3	**DISCIPLINE**	Fair agreements between employers and employees.
4	**UNITY OF COMMAND**	Clear recognition of one person giving orders to reduce tension.
5	**UNITY OF DIRECTION**	One person planning for group activities with a shared objective.

6	SUBORDINATION OF INDIVIDUAL TO GROUP INTEREST	Ensures employees achieve organisational goals rather than their own.
7	REMUNERATION	Pay should be fair to employees and organisations.
8	CENTRALISATION	Incorporating both centralisation and decentralisation in order to achieve organisational goals more efficiently.
9	SCALAR CHAIN	The line of authority from top to bottom of organisations.
10	ORDER	The right people at the right place for the right job.
11	EQUITY	Fair treatment of all employees.
12	STABILITY OF TENURE	Reducing inefficiency by having stable tenure (for example, permanent jobs or long-term contracts).
13	INITIATIVE	All employees encouraged to show initiative.
14	*ESPRIT DE CORPS* (TEAM SPIRIT)	Contacts within and between departments should be encouraged.

Table 1.3 Fayol's fourteen principles of management

Max Weber and the ideal–typical bureaucracy

Max Weber (1984–1920) was a German sociologist, rather than a practising manager like Taylor or Fayol. Weber took up the scientific management idea that there is 'one best way' to do a job and argued that there must be 'one best way' to run an organisation. He was particularly interested in managing the total organisation and in examining the structure of organisations and investigating why employees obey those in authority. Weber was not the first theorist to use the term **bureaucracy**, but in his writings he detailed the attributes of bureaucracy that still exist today (Table 1.4). The word bureaucracy comes from the word bureau, used from the early eighteenth century in Western Europe not just to refer to a writing desk, but to an office, i.e. a workplace, where officials worked. Weber suggested the need for impersonal and rational management in charge of a bureaucratic organisation.

DIVISION OF LABOUR	Clear definitions of authority and responsibility as official duties.
ORGANISATION OF POSITIONS INTO A HIERARCHY	With each under the authority of a higher position.
PEOPLE ARE ASSIGNED TO POSITIONS IN THE HIERARCHY	According to qualifications, assessment by examination or training and experience.
DECISIONS AND ACTIONS ARE RECORDED IN WRITING	With files providing continuity and memory over time.
MANAGEMENT AND OWNERSHIP	Are separated.
ALL ARE SUBJECT TO RULES AND PROCEDURES	Applied impersonally and equally to all to ensure predictable behaviour.

Table 1.4 Weber's elements of bureaucracy

Weber believed that bureaucracy was necessary for the needs of large-scale organisations, enabling organisations to be both more efficient and adaptable to change. He believed in the *rational–legal model* of an organisation: **rational** because managers made decisions according to clear criteria; and **legal** because those in authority were appointed by a legitimate process. Bureaucracy, however, has become associated with 'red tape', for example, excessive rules and paperwork leading to inefficiency. It is important to remember that Weber's emphasis was on improving efficiency and this was suitable for organisations at that time, whereas modern organisations are more concerned with issues such as innovation and flexibility.

Assessment of the classical management perspective

The classical perspective deserves credit for focusing serious attention on the importance of effective management. Many of the concepts developed during this era, such as job specialisation, time and motion studies, and scientific methods are still used today. On the other hand, these early theorists often took a simplistic view of management and failed to understand the human element of organisations.

Contributions

- Laid the foundation for later developments in management theory.
- Identified important management processes, functions and skills that are still recognised as such today.
- Focused attention on management as a valid subject of scientific inquiry.

Limitations

- More appropriate for stable and simple organisations than for today's dynamic and complex organisations.
- Often prescribed universal procedures that are not appropriate in some settings.
- Employees were generally viewed as tools rather than resources.

The human relations perspective

As outlined above, the classical management perspective emphasised organisational structures, and many classical management theorists viewed employees as part of the mechanics of organisations. In contrast, the human relations and social psychological theorists emphasised the importance of the human factor at work. In particular, individual attitudes and behaviours of groups were regarded as important. Human relations theorists were concerned with the motivation of employees, suggesting that employees are motivated by factors other than pay. Motivation is discussed in Chapter 7. The **Hawthorne studies**, some of the most significant studies supporting the behavioural management perspective, were carried out by **Elton Mayo** and his associates between 1927 and 1932 at the Hawthorne plant of the Western Electric Company in Chicago. The emphasis in the Hawthorne studies was on the worker rather than on the work. The studies involved manipulating lighting for one group of workers (experimental group) and comparing productivity in that group with another group's productivity where the lighting was not changed. Interestingly, productivity continued to increase in both groups, even when the lighting for the experimental group was decreased. The main conclusions to be drawn from the Hawthorne studies are:

- The need to belong to a group in the workplace is much more important than previous theorists had realised.
- Individual workers cannot be treated in isolation and must be seen as members of a group.
- Managers and employers need to be aware of the social needs of employees in organisations and to cater for those needs.

- Belonging to a group and having recognition within that group is as important as monetary incentives or good physical working conditions.

The emphasis on employee social or belonging needs in contrast to the tasks to be fulfilled began during this era and are still considered to be very important in organisations today.

The Hawthorne experiment began as a study into physical working conditions, but developed as a series of studies into social factors, such as membership of groups and relationships with supervisors. As a result of the Hawthorne studies, the emphasis in organisations during the 1930s and 1940s changed from being task- or work-oriented to highlighting the social or belonging needs of employees. These concepts are still emphasised in management theories today. Further expansions of these theories during the 1950s and 1960s by early motivational theorists, such as Maslow, McGregor, Herzberg and McClelland, suggested that employees have far more than just physical and social needs to be satisfied. These theories are dealt with in detail in Chapter 7.

Mary Parker Follett

Mary Parker Follett (1868–1933) was an American social worker, management consultant and pioneer in the fields of organisational theory and organisational behaviour. Her ideas on negotiation, power and employee participation were highly influential in the development of the fields of organisational studies, alternative dispute resolution and the human relations movement.

Mary Parker Follett stressed the interactions of management and workers. She looked at management and leadership holistically, and she identified a leader as someone who sees the whole rather than the particular. Follett was one of the first (and for a long time, one of the few) to integrate the idea of organisational conflict into management theory, and is sometimes considered the 'mother of conflict resolution'.

Follett suggested that organisations function on the principle of power 'with' and not power 'over' and recommended the creation of power-sharing arrangements in organisations. She was also a pioneer of community centres — public locations where members of a community may gather for group activities, social support, public information, and other purposes. Follett's work, therefore, set the stage for effective, progressive changes in management philosophy which were brought about through the humanisation of the workplace.

Chester Barnard

Chester Barnard (1886–1961) was a formidable part of Mayo's human relations movement, even before Mayo became famous. Barnard had suggested that managers need to know more about human behaviour, and, in particular, more about the informal groups of an organisation, especially the relationships between workers and outsiders. He stressed short, direct lines of communication, vertical interaction that was persuasive and overcame differences.

Barnard observed that while orders given by management to employees are certainly significant, the Hawthorne Studies pointed out that this is not always enough. Workers must also be willing to obey. Thus, he believed that a certain amount of co-operation between management and employees is necessary. Authority is not all that is necessary, as the classical schools of management would have suggested. Barnard reinforced what became a fundamental idea in organisational theory: that all organisations possess both a *formal* organisation and an *informal* organisation. Barnard asserted that the informal organisation regulates how and even if employees will obey management orders and instructions. Based upon this contention, he taught that there are basically only three types of orders that can be given by managers to employees:

- First, are orders that are unquestionably acceptable and that are always obeyed because they lie within what Barnard called the employee's zone of indifference, or typically dealt with things that are part of an employee's job description and are routine.
- Second, are orders that may or may not be followed, depending upon the employee and the conduct accepted by the employee's informal organisation because such orders come close to being unacceptable.
- Third, are orders that are completely unacceptable and that will always be disobeyed because these kinds of orders go way beyond an employee's zone of indifference.

Barnard's perspective was similar to that of Mary Parker Follett and was unusual for his time. He argued that managers should obtain authority by treating subordinates with respect and competence.

Assessment of human relations perspective

The human relations perspective focuses on employee behaviour in an organisational context. The human relations movement supplanted scientific management as the dominant approach to management in the 1930s and 1940s.

Contributions

- Provided important insights into motivation, group dynamics and other interpersonal processes in organisations.
- Focused managerial attention on these processes.
- Challenged the view that employees are tools and furthered the belief that employees are valuable resources.

Limitations

- The complexity of individual behaviour makes prediction of that behaviour difficult.
- Many behavioural concepts have not yet been put to use because some managers are reluctant to adopt them.

The quantitative management perspective

Another management perspective, which emerged during the Second World War, was known as the quantitative management perspective. During this period, scientists and mathematicians solved military problems by using resources more efficiently and effectively. The achievements of this approach were also applied to organisations. Quantitative management concentrates on using mathematical and statistical models, and more recently computers, to achieve organisational efficiency and effectiveness. Quantitative management may be further subdivided into *management science* and *operations management*.

Management science involves the development of mathematical models and manipulating data to produce results. Management science also helps to solve organisational problems by using mixed teams of specialists who analyse problems and suggest various options by using complex statistical data in order to obtain greater understanding of problems. Management science encourages decision-making, based on the use of models, to obtain greater effectiveness. This has been facilitated recently by the use of special computer packages.

Operations management is a transformation process that can be considered as a form of applied management science and is used (Naylor 2004):

> to plan, organise, operate and control a transformation system that takes inputs from a variety of sources and produces outputs of goods and services at times and places defined by internal or external customers.

Operations management is concerned with making entire organisations more effective and efficient from the strategic management level down to the operating level. Operations management techniques can be applied to a wide range of activities, including forecasting, inventory management and managing queues. Overall, quantitative management has provided managers with a number of decision-making tools and techniques which are particularly useful for planning and controlling and has increased understanding of overall organisational processes. It is important, however, to remember that mathematical models cannot predict or account for individual employee behaviour and attitude.

The **systems approach** is a management theory built around the idea of systems. A *system* is an interrelated set of elements functioning as a whole. The systems approach suggests that managers should focus on the role each part (or department) of an organisation plays in the whole organisation, rather than dealing separately with each part. The systems approach recognises the different needs of various departments; for example, the production manager may want to produce a variety of products, whereas the marketing manager may prefer to concentrate on one or two specialised products, and the finance manager may be primarily concerned with keeping costs to a minimum. The systems approach stresses the importance of *subsystems* — systems within a broader system. The finance, production and marketing departments are not only systems in their own right but are also subsystems within an organisation. *Synergy* emphasises the interrelationships between all parts of an organisation, reflecting that organisational departments (or subsystems) may often be more successful working together than working alone. This suggests that departments and units in a business are more productive when they work together than when they operate separately.

The systems approach, therefore, means that managers have to discuss the various requirements of each department in terms of meeting the needs of the whole organisation. This interaction requires a high degree of communication and the breaking down of barriers between various departments and functions of an organisation. Griffin (2008) suggests that when organisations are viewed as systems, four basic elements can be identified:

- inputs
- transformation processes
- outputs
- feedback.

First, inputs are the resources an organisation gets from its environment, including raw materials, information, and financial and human resources. Second, through managerial and technological processes the inputs are transformed into outputs. Outputs include flows of information, materials and human energy which move through a system and are transformed by various processes into products and services. Finally, feedback is the process of monitoring information about systems in order to evaluate their operation.

Assessment of the quantitative management perspective

The quantitative management perspective has provided managers with an abundance of decision-making tools and techniques and has increased understanding of overall organisational processes. It focuses on applying mathematical models and processes to management situations.

Contributions

- Developed sophisticated quantitative techniques to assist in decision-making.
- Application of models has increased awareness and understanding of complex organisational processes and situations.
- Useful in the planning and controlling processes.

Limitations

- Cannot fully explain or predict the behaviour of people in organisations.
- Mathematical sophistication may come at the expense of other important skills.

The contingency management perspective

Theorists from the classical management perspective believed that there was 'one best way' to manage organisations and once this 'best way' was found all could learn from it. In contrast, the contingency management perspective suggests that there is no 'one best way' to manage organisations, and aims to provide solutions to organisational management problems by responding to the unique circumstances involved. Research conducted in the 1960s and 1970s focused on situational factors that affected the appropriate structure of organisations and the appropriate leadership styles for different situations. This type of perspective recognises that in each situation there are common circumstances (those previously experienced by other organisations) *and* unique circumstances, and these may be looked at in combination to provide better solutions for particular problems. When a problem is examined, its solution will depend on its particular causes. The task for contingency management is to identify which solutions are most likely to work in given circumstances. The contingency management perspective has developed from attempts to apply various techniques to solve management problems, for example, using the theories of the behavioural management perspective (with regard to motivation) together with quantitative analyses of findings.

Four important ideas of contingency theory are:

1. There is no universal or one best way to manage.
2. The design of an organisation and its subsystems must 'fit' with the environment.
3. Effective organisations not only have a proper 'fit' with the environment but also between its subsystems.
4. The needs of an organisation are better satisfied when it is properly designed and the management style is appropriate both to the tasks undertaken and the nature of the work group.

Using the contingency management approach, managers consider the objectives of a particular action, the people involved, the equipment available, and internal and external conditions. Internal and external environments are dealt with in detail in Chapter 2. A number of theorists, such as Burns and Stalker, Lawrence and Lorsch, and Mintzberg, have studied links between organisational structures and other variables.

Burns and Stalker

From the late 1950s, British behavioural scientists Tom Burns and G.M. Stalker have examined how organisations adjust to changing environmental conditions. Burns and Stalker characterised organisations as being mechanistic organisations or organic organisations. **Mechanistic organisations** tend to have rigid structures and can be similar to bureaucracies. **Organic organisations**, in contrast, tend to be flexible in structure and adaptive to change (see Table 1.5 for a summary of the characteristics). Many organisations, however, would lie somewhere between the two extremes.

MECHANISTIC	ORGANIC
Tasks are specialised, precise and narrow.	Tasks are more independent and imprecise.
Tasks tend to be rigid, unless altered formally by top management.	Tasks are adjusted and redefined by employees.
Information relevant to particular situations and running the organisation lies with the chief executive.	Information is generated throughout the organisation.
Communication is usually between superior and subordinate (vertical) in relation to issuing orders and instructions.	Communication is both vertical and horizontal (between peers) and is used for information and advice.
Loyalty to the organisation and obedience to superiors is expected.	Loyalty is to project and teamwork.

Table 1.5 Characteristics of mechanistic and organic organisations

Burns and Stalker suggested that they did not view one or other system as being superior, but that organisations could move from one system to the other as external organisational conditions changed. They believed that what was important was gaining the most appropriate system for the particular circumstances.

Lawrence and Lorsch

The work of Paul Lawrence and Jay Lorsch, first published in the United States in 1967, was influenced by Burns and Stalker. Their study began with an investigation of the degree of **differentiation** (dividing organisations into functions such as production, sales, finance, etc.) and **integration** (achieving collaboration between departments to achieve overall unity) within six organisations in the plastics industry and their rapidly changing environments.

Lawrence and Lorsch believed that both mechanistic *and* organic types of organisations were crucial for coping with environmental diversity, whereas Burns and Stalker believed that organic systems were more appropriate for changing conditions. Lawrence and Lorsch suggested that, in rapidly changing environmental situations, large organisations still have to maintain structure and formality. They also believed that most organisations are in a state of tension as a result of the need to be both differentiated and integrated.

Henry Mintzberg

Henry Mintzberg developed his concept of an organisation structure composed of various segments (summarised in Figure 1.2).

Mintzberg contends that six basic components are found in organisations:

- the *strategic apex* running the whole organisation
- the *middle-line managers* connecting the operating core with the apex
- the *technostructure* designing and controlling processes, for example, engineers, information specialists, accountants
- the *support staff* providing direct services, for example, public relations, transport, canteen, cleaning
- the *operating core* producing goods or services
- the *ideology* binding the whole together.

According to Mintzberg each organisation is dominated by a different component part, for example, the owner–manager entrepreneurial organisation is dominated by the strategic apex. In contrast, a highly skilled professional organisation, such as a law firm, works directly on its output.

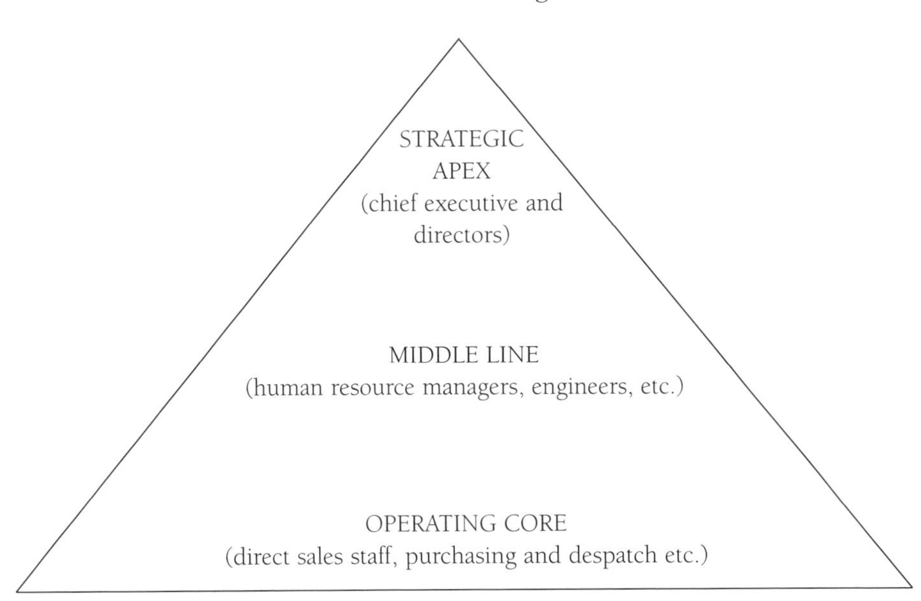

Figure 1.2 Mintzberg's model of an organisation structure

Peters and Waterman

Thomas Peters and Robert Waterman investigated sixty-two major American organisations that had performed excellently during the period 1961 to 1980. Their book, *In Search of Excellence: Lessons from America's Best-run Companies*, shows eight management excellence characteristics not generally shown by organisations that did not perform as well:

- a bias for action — moving on rather than being slowed by analysis
- closeness to the customer — learning from the people served
- autonomy and entrepreneurship — fostering innovators and risk takers
- productivity through people — participation as a basis for rising standards
- a hands-on, value-driven approach — all stakeholders know what the company stands for, leaders get involved at all levels
- sticking to the knitting — focusing on business known to participants
- a simple form, lean staff — a minimum of headquarters staff to run a large business through simpler organisation structures
- simultaneous loose–tight properties — being as decentralised as possible while centralising the things that really matter.

Managers are now encouraged to recognise the ability of the people they manage and to devolve decision-making as far as possible. This suggests that the people who have to implement a decision should make it by analysing the situation and deciding on courses of action. This should result in the contingency approach being carried to successful conclusions.

It is clear that the contingency management approach needs to analyse each situation and then draw on various schools of management theory in order to decide on the most appropriate combination. The contingency approach helps managers to be aware of the complexity in any situation and to take an active role in trying to determine what would work best in each situation, against the background of rapidly changing external environments.

Peter Drucker

Peter Drucker (1909–2005) was a writer, teacher and management consultant. In 1959, he coined the term 'knowledge worker' (see Chapter 10). He was interested in the growing effect of people who worked with their minds rather than their hands. Drucker predicted that the major changes in society would be brought about by information. He argued that *knowledge* has become the central, key resource that knows no geography. According to him, the largest working group will become what he calls *knowledge workers*. The defining characteristic of these knowledge workers is the level of their formal education. Thus, education and development, and to some degree training, will be the central concern of a knowledge society.

Several ideas run through most of Drucker's writings:

- *Decentralisation and simplification.* He discounted the command and control model and asserted that companies work best when they are decentralised. He believed that organisations tend to produce too many products, hire employees they do not need (when a better solution would be outsourcing), and expand into economic sectors that they should avoid.
- *Respect of the worker.* He believed that employees are assets and not liabilities. He taught that knowledge workers are the essential ingredients of the modern economy. Central to this philosophy is the view that people are an organisation's most valuable resource and that a manager's job is to prepare employees to perform.
- *The need for community.* He suggested that volunteering in the non-profit sector was the key to fostering a healthy society where people found a sense of belonging and civic pride.
- *A company's primary responsibility is to serve its customers.* Profit is not the primary goal, but rather an essential condition for the company's continued existence.

Drucker cared not just about how business manages its resources, but also how public and private organisations operate morally and ethically within society. He respected the values of education, personal responsibility and businesses' accountability to society.

Chris Argyris

Chris Argyris is an American business theorist, and is known for work in the area of learning organisations (see Chapter 10). He advocates an approach to research that focuses on generating knowledge that is useful in solving practical problems. He has influenced thinking about the relationship of organisational learning and action research. He explored the impact of formal organisational structures, control systems and management on individuals and how they responded and adapted to them.

Argyris observed that organisational goals and the personal goals of employees are (usually) in conflict. In the formal organisation, he believes that employees are expected to be passive and subordinate, to accept little control over their work, to have a short-term outlook and are expected to produce under conditions leading to psychological failure. He argued for less structured forms of organisation that enabled people to express themselves within a company, not just to conform to it. He believes that most organisations were run on the basis of coercive power which tends to make them rigid. He calls for organisations to be run on the basis of knowledgeable groups and says that the matrix organisation is designed less around power and more around who has the relevant information.

Finally, towards the end of the twentieth century, management tended to be subdivided into separate branches, such as:

- human resource management
- operations management or production management
- strategic management
- marketing management
- financial management
- information technology management or management information systems.

At the beginning of the twenty-first century, however, observers find it increasingly difficult to subdivide management into functional categories in this way. Several more processes simultaneously involve various categories. Branches of management theory also exist in relation to non-profit organisations and to government organisations such as public administration, public management and educational management.

Classical management, late 1890s until 1914	
Taylor	Scientific management
Gantt	The Gantt chart
Gilbreth and Gilbreth	Motion study
Fayol	Management principles
Weber	Bureaucracy
Behavioural management, 1900 to 1940	
Mayo	Hawthorne studies
McGregor	Theory X, Theory Y (see Chapter 7)
Maslow	Hierarchy of needs (see Chapter 7)
Quantitative management 1940+	Management science Operations management
Contingency management 1980+	Organisational behaviour
Burns and Stalker	Mechanistic and organic organisations
Lawrence and Lorsch	Differentiation and integration of organisations
Mintzberg	Organisational structure
Peters and Waterman	Characteristics of excellent organisations
Drucker	Knowledge workers
Argyris	Learning organisations
Follett	Conflict resolution
Barnard	Informed organisational groups

Table 1.6 Summary of management theories

1.4 Key points

Management is a set of functions directed at achieving organisational goals efficiently and effectively. These basic functions include:

- planning
- decision-making
- organising
- leading
- controlling.

Modern-day management theories have emerged from a combination of approaches to management which were developed over the last one hundred years.

The *classical management* perspective consisted of scientific management and administrative management. Overall, the classical management perspective was concerned with improving organisational efficiency and work methods for individual workers but had little regard for employees.

The *human relations* perspective was concerned with individual and group behaviour. This perspective emerged primarily as a result of the Hawthorne studies. The approach recognised the importance of group behaviour for employees in organisations and highlighted the fact that employees are also motivated by non-monetary factors.

The *quantitative management* perspective consists of management science and operations management. This perspective applies quantitative techniques in attempting to solve problems and make decisions.

The *contingency management* perspective suggests that there is no universal approach to managing organisations, as organisational management depends on (or is contingent upon) each individual situation. Contingency management theorists are concerned with the links between organisational structures and other variables together with many other modern-day management issues (these issues are discussed in detail in Chapter 10).

Important terms and concepts

bureaucracy (p.9)
classical management perspective (p.4)
commanding (p.2)
contingency management perspective (p.16)
controlling (p.2)
co-ordinating (p.2)
effective (p.2)
efficient (p.2)
Fayol's principles of management (p.8)
first-line managers (p.3)
forecasting (p.1)
Gantt chart (p.7)
Hawthorne studies (p.11)
human relations perspective (p.11)
knowledge workers (p. 20)
learning organisation (p. 21)
management defined (p.1)

management science (p.14)
mechanistic organisation (p.17)
middle managers (p.3)
Mintzberg's organisational types (p.18)
operations management (p.14)
organic organisation (p.17)
organising (p.2)
planning (p.1)
quantitative management perspective (p.14)
systems approach (p. 15)
Taylor's principles of scientific management (p.5)
top managers (p.3)
Weber's elements of bureaucracy (p.10)

Questions for review

1. Critically compare and contrast the contributions made by the classical management perspective and the behavioural management perspective. Include the primary contributors to each of these theories.

2. Illustrate the importance of forecasting, planning, organising, co-ordinating and controlling for an organisation with which you are familiar.

3. Discuss the relevance of Fayol's principles of management for modern organisations.

4. Write brief notes on the following:
   a. The Hawthorne studies
   b. Bureaucracy
   c. Quantitative management perspective
   d. Contingency management perspective.

5. Do you think that workers are prepared to put up with dull, boring jobs if they are paid high wages?

2
THE ORGANISATIONAL ENVIRONMENT

Objectives

This chapter will help you to:

- describe the main forces of the external environment and show how they impact on organisations
- describe the main forces of the internal (or task) environment and show how they impact on organisations
- explain how Porter's 'five forces' determine industry profitability
- understand Porter's 'three generic strategies'.

2.1 The organisational environment defined

All societies are influenced by managers and their organisations. Managers need to have a clear understanding of the environment in which their organisations function. Organisations include:

- hospitals
- schools
- government agencies
- businesses
- voluntary groups
- religious groups.

An organisation has been defined (Griffin 2008) as:

> a group of people working together in a structured and co-ordinated fashion to achieve a set of goals.

All organisations interact with the environment in which they operate. Everything that customers, companies and other institutions do will have some impact on the environment. The environment is composed of a number of elements that can determine the success or failure of an organisation. The environment of an organisation may be defined as: *all those elements that lie outside and inside the organisation's boundary with which the organisation interacts*. From this definition it is apparent that an organisation operates in both an **external** (or **macro**) and **internal** (or **task**) environment. An organisation can also operate in an **international** environment.

2.2 The external environment

The external environment consists of elements that lie outside an organisation and have the potential to influence that organisation in significant ways (see Figure 2.1). Organisations cannot determine external environmental factors, such as a nation's recession or boom period. The external environment comprises elements that can be divided into four main groupings, known by the acronym **STEP**:

- the **social** environment
- the **technological** environment
- the **economic** environment
- the **political–legal** environment.

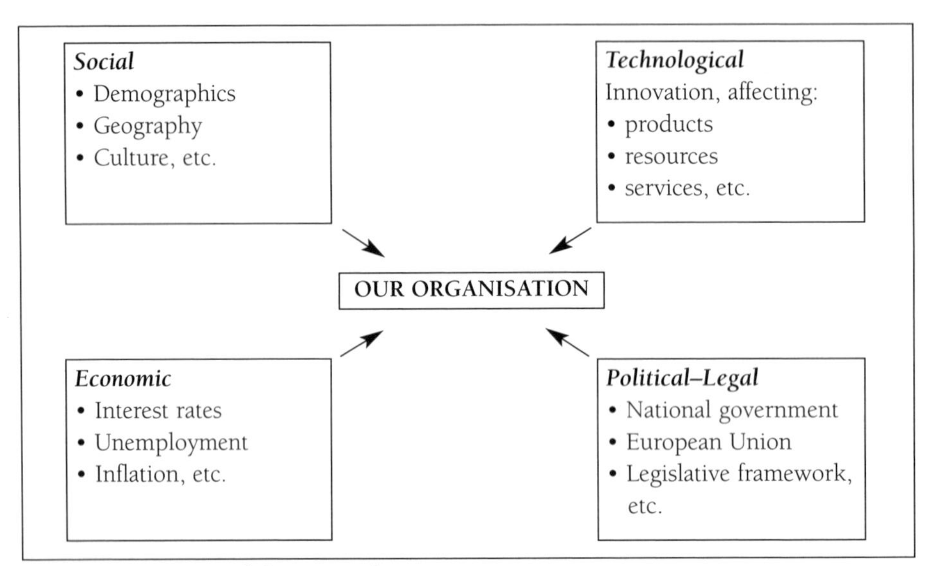

Figure 2.1 Forces of the external environment

The social environment

The social, societal or sociocultural environment refers to the elements that generally make up society. These elements include the *demographic, geographic* and *cultural factors* in which an organisation operates. Social processes influence organisations in servicing demands for products and services, and also influence standards of organisational conduct according to the respective societal values in which differing organisations operate. The social environment, however, can go through significant changes, even over a decade. Immigration is acknowledged to be one of the most powerful social forces affecting a society. Ireland had been a country of mass emigration for centuries; but Ireland's economic boom during the 1990s brought unprecedented levels of prosperity and transformed it into a country of net immigration by the early 2000s. For the first time in its history, Ireland experienced a significant inflow of migrants — both workers and asylum seekers — from outside the European Union and, as a consequence, the population of Ireland is more ethnically diverse than at any previous time (see Chapter 10).

Demographic factors include:

- population
- age structure
- income distribution.

Population changes affect the demand for products and services, for example, as the average expected life span is now greater than in previous generations, the supply of health care and related products for the elderly has greatly increased. The shift in population from Irish rural areas to cities also affects infrastructural services, such as transport, housing and schools. *Age structure* also has an influence on an organisation's environment; for example, during a baby boom period the demand for child-related products and services increases. *Income distribution* also influences the environmental factors of an organisation; for example, the demand for luxury items and non-essential services increases when the members of the society in which an organisation operates have more disposable income.

Geographic factors, for example:

- transport infrastructure
- climate
- sources of energy
- language

have an influence on the operations of an organisation. In Ireland, for instance, many organisations are based close to the sea ports and airports of Dublin, Cork and Shannon, and many American organisations prefer to set up operations within the European Union in the English-speaking environments of Ireland or Britain.

Cultural factors, such as:

- values
- social norms

- the prevailing attitudes of a population

also affect the environment in which an organisation operates. Differences in culture arise from gender, social class, education, religious background and age. National culture in all countries remains very strong, and successful managers have to be prepared to adapt to local environments. Attitudes and social values which determine a culture are constantly changing in all countries, and managers also have to be adaptable to these changing factors.

The technological environment

According to Griffin (2008), a technological environment refers to the methods available for converting resources into products or services. Technology affects the operation of internal organisational environments, and relies on the technology that is available in external environments. Technological environments are rapidly changing, with noticeable advances in organisations, varying from barcode scanning systems in the commodity industry to video-conferencing and e-mailing facilities for transnational communication. Organisations which have introduced loyalty cards, use this method to collect detailed information on subscribing customers, as well as rewarding customers according to the amount they spend.

Since the early 1990s, there has been an explosive growth in the number of organisations using the World Wide Web to market products and services, taking advantage of the exponential growth in the widespread use of the Internet. According to Eurostat (2009), nearly three-quarters of the EU population aged 16–24 used the Internet daily or almost daily in the first quarter of 2009, compared with 58 per cent of Irish individuals aged 16–24. The Eurostat survey showed that Ireland is number ten in the world for online shopping and has one of the fastest growth rates in online purchases in Europe (http://ec.europa.eu).

The economic environment

The economic dimension of the external environment refers to the overall conditions in which an organisation operates. The economic environment influences the costs of operating in different locations, for example, the cost of labour in a particular country. Other factors that influence the economic environment include:

- inflation
- interest rates
- unemployment
- per capita income.

The economic boom which Ireland experienced from the late 1990s resulted in low unemployment and an 'employees' market', where employers faced additional difficulties in finding and retaining suitable employees, as employees had the choice to move more often from one place of employment to another. In contrast, and more recently, however, according to the Central Statistics Office (2009) unemployment levels reached 11.6 per cent. The biggest fall in employment was in the construction sector, with wholesale and retail categories also recording big drops in the number of people employed (www.cso.ie).

The economic environment is also important for service industries, such as restaurants, cinemas and theatres, because in an economic boom consumers make use of these services more frequently and in greater numbers. Charitable and non-profit organisations are also affected by the economic environment and its effect on people's disposable income.

The political–legal environment

The political–legal environment refers to government regulations imposed on organisations and the legal framework established for operations. In Ireland, organisations operate under Irish and European Union laws. Within the European Union, member states have to adhere to common decisions on, for example, fishing, agriculture, trade, economics and the physical environment. Laws that affect human resource managers include:

- recruitment (for example, being an equal opportunities employer)
- minimum wages
- parental leave
- unfair dismissals
- employment permits
- employment contracts
- redundancy
- protection of part-time employees.

The political stability and political relationships of a country also affect organisations when expansion into certain countries is planned.

2.3 The internal environment

The internal environment is also referred to as the *operating environment* or the *task environment*. Factors that are part of the internal environment which affect organisational behaviour include:

- customers

- competitors
- suppliers
- distributors
- investors
- trade unions.

Customers

Managers have to decide about two fundamental questions:
- *What business are we in?*
- *Who are our customers?*

And when an organisation begins to ask itself:
- *What 'line of business' are we actually in?*

it is beginning to identify its potential customers.

By asking these questions it is clear that an organisation is identifying **marketing** as an important management function. Once the organisation understands the business it is in, doing what it is good at ('sticking to the knitting') becomes clear. The organisation can then begin to segment and target the various markets and then position its product(s) for those customers it wishes to serve. A **market segment** is a subset of a market made up of people or organisations sharing one or more characteristics that cause them to demand similar products and/or services based on the qualities of those products such as price or function. A **target market** is the market segment that a particular product is marketed to. It is often defined by age, gender and/or socioeconomic grouping. An organisation's customers can include:
- individuals — who may be buying products for their own consumption
- other companies — who may be interested in buying raw materials
- government departments.

It is important for an organisation to know its customers in order to meet their requirements by having *the right product, at the right place, at the right time*. It is important for marketing managers to know their customers, not only who they are but also what influences customer purchasing decisions, as well as knowing customer disposable incomes and lifestyles. This could range from millions of customers if starting an online business, to a few thousand individuals if opening a retail store in a small town. Feargal Quinn of Superquinn noted that it is not enough to satisfy one's customers — an organisation must be able to 'delight' its customers (Quinn 2002).

Competitors

The competitors of an organisation are other organisations that compete with it for revenue. As organisations operating in the same industry compete for the same customers, managers must anticipate and react to the strategies of competitors in order to remain competitive. Competition in the Irish supermarket industry, for example, has increased with the entrance of Aldi and Lidl, offering a competitively priced but more limited range of goods. Price, however, is not the only element that influences customers and competitors in the supermarket industry, for example Dunnes Stores Ltd competes using slogans such as: 'The difference is we're Irish'. Other factors that competitors use to win customers include:

- quality
- reliability
- responsiveness
- service
- speed of delivery.

Suppliers

Suppliers are organisations that provide resources for other organisations. Supplies vary and can include:

- capital goods
- vehicles
- equipment
- raw materials
- finance
- personnel, provided through agencies or by subcontract.

Most organisations use several suppliers simultaneously as having a sole supplier brings with it a higher risk if that company goes out of business. Losing a key supplier of raw materials can mean that production flow is interrupted or a lower quality product or more expensive substitution has to be made. Choosing suppliers, negotiating terms and building professional working relationship are tasks that managers have to perform frequently.

Distributors

Distribution involves handling and moving out-bound goods from an organisation to customers. Distribution may be direct, using company-owned transport, or indirect, using external agents or brokers. The distributors' task is to ensure that the right product will be at the right place at the right time, and the choice of distribution channel is determined by the needs of customers as well as by knowledge of particular markets. The choice of distributors also has to be consistent with the needs and capabilities of an organisation. The computer firm Dell is an example of an organisation which uses direct selling in order to attract customers in a very competitive industry sector.

Investors

Investors include banks and other financial institutions, which provide short-term finance to shareholders, or lenders of long-term capital who have a long-term commitment.

Trade unions

A **trade union** is an organisation of workers who have come together to achieve common goals in key areas such as working conditions. The trade union, through its leadership, bargains with the employer on behalf of union members and negotiates labour contracts with employers. Terms may include the negotiation of wages, work rules, complaint procedures, rules governing hiring, dismissing, and promotion of workers, benefits, and workplace safety and policies. The agreements negotiated by the union leaders are binding on members and the employer and in some cases on other non-member workers.

According to Wallace *et al.* (2004), trade unions are seen as an effective means of achieving satisfactory pay and working conditions for employees. Trade unions aim to ensure that employees are treated fairly by employers. The basic strength of a trade union lies in its ability to organise and unite workers. The main objectives of trade unions are to:

- achieve satisfactory levels of pay and conditions of employment
- provide members with a range of services
- strengthen employee bargaining power by replacing individual bargaining with collective bargaining
- reflect the interests of wage earners or workers.

Figure 2.2 illustrates the different factors within the external and internal organisational environments.

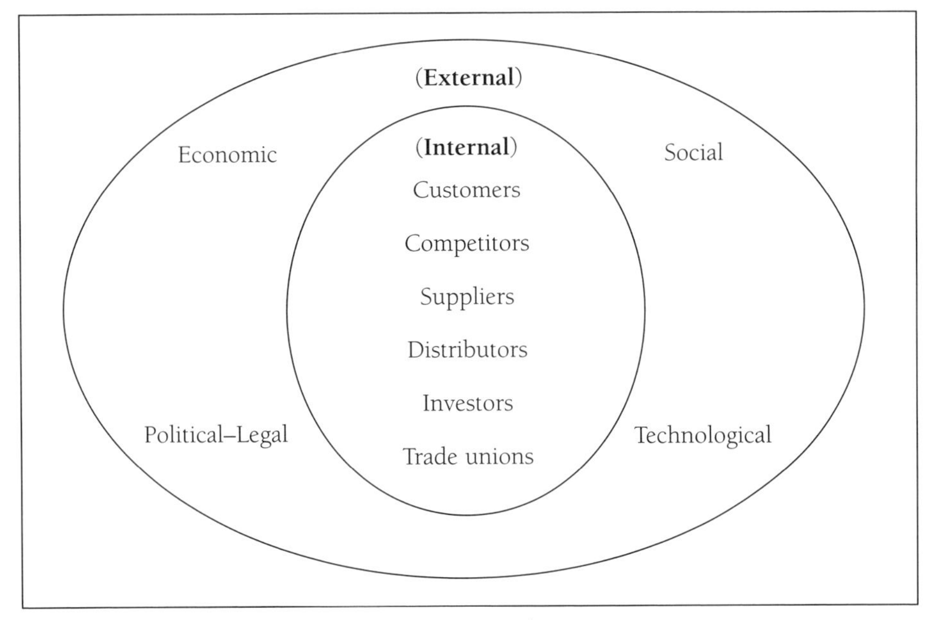

Figure 2.2 External and internal organisational environments

2.4 The international environment

The international environment of an organisation is concerned with operating across national boundaries. As trade barriers, geographic boundaries and political borders come down the opportunities for many organisations are increasing. Within the international environment there are multiple economic, social, cultural, legal, political and technological environments. Managers have to make decisions, for example, regarding currency, shipping costs, import duties and other taxes. Operating in the international environment, therefore, is far more complex than operating domestically. Organisations that operate internationally need to pay special attention to varying sociocultural factors, social structures and customs.

Griffin (2008) views the international environment as the extent to which an organisation is involved in or is affected by business in other countries. Organisations that operate in only one country can also be affected by the international environment as they may face competition from foreign imports or may find it necessary to import raw materials to manufacture their product(s). For many Irish organisations the international environment is of increasing importance for both exporting and importing products.

The transfer of employees from their home countries to host countries to work for a number of years is another aspect that many human resource managers have to deal with. The preparation, recruitment, selection and training both of staff members and their family members are some of the issues that have to be dealt with when employees move internationally.

In the European context, co-operation in trade and economic policies has an influence on Irish management policies. Ireland's participation in the European Union means that Irish laws and customs are affected by European Union laws, guidelines and decisions. The single European market has also opened up many opportunities for Irish organisations.

2.5 The competitive environment

The performance of an organisation will be influenced by the structure of the particular industry in which it operates as this affects the level of competition in that product market; for example, Cadbury's, Terry's and Nestlé are among the competition overlaps in the chocolate market. Porter (1980) suggested that, to be successful, *an organisation needs to gain competitive advantage* over competitors. **Competitive advantage** means being different or doing something better than the opposition in a way that is important to target customers. Organisations might differentiate themselves from competitors by offering similar products at lower prices or, instead, organisations might differentiate themselves by supplying prestige products with higher quality than the quality of opposition products. Bailey's Irish Cream, for example, created a completely new market where no similar product existed previously and it is now one of the top twenty spirit brands in the world. It was named the world's top-selling liqueur brand in 1998. According to its manufacturers its competitive advantage since its launch in 1974 has been: 'an original product and a taste of Ireland'.

The effective management of human resources can also be a source of competitive advantage for an organisation, for example, contented and hard-working employees are more likely to produce excellent work that adds value to their organisation. While many organisations attempt to imitate the competitive advantage of their opposition, imitating employee behaviour of opponents is, however, a difficult task. Overall, the task for managers is first to create a competitive advantage and then to sustain that advantage. According to Barney (1996), a **sustained competitive advantage** is a competitive advantage that exists after all attempts at strategic imitation have ceased.

Porter's five forces

Michael Porter, of Harvard Business School, has taken competitive advantage as his focus in developing corporate strategy. Porter emphasises the impact of external environments on an organisation. He suggests that there are five major influences or forces which impact on an organisation's ability to compete and which determine industry profitability (see Figure 2.3):

- rivalry among existing competitors
- threat of substitute products and services
- threat of new entrants
- bargaining power of suppliers
- bargaining power of customers.

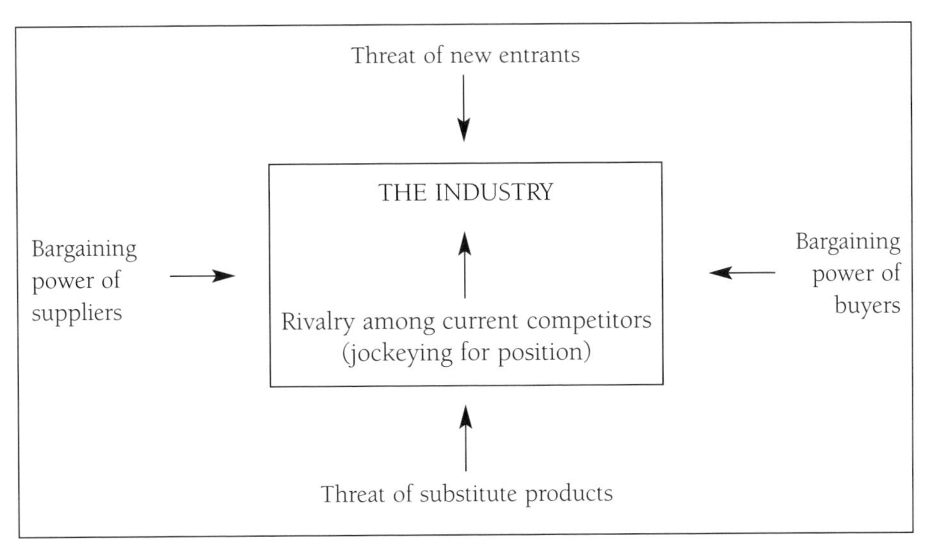

Figure 2.3 Porter's five forces model of competition

1. **Competitive rivalry** is intense when there are many competitors operating in the same industry. Rivalry among competitors may appear in terms of advertising, price, quality, increased customer service and product differentiation. An organisation needs to decide with whom it is really competing and to be aware of the main threats emerging from competitors. Competitive rivalry is intense in the soft drinks market, for example, the 'cola wars' between Pepsi-Cola, Coca-Cola and supermarkets' own-brand cola.

2. **The threat of substitutes** is more powerful where there are alternatives and substitutes for a company's products. Organisations, therefore, not only compete with other organisations providing similar products but also compete with organisations which provide substitute products. In

the soft drinks sector, for example, Ballygowan not only competes with other bottled water producers, such as Tipperary or Perrier, but also with Irish Spring, Club and Seven-Up.

3. **The threat of new entrants** is the extent to which new competitors can enter a market. Potential new entrants to an industry have more difficulty in setting up a high-capital-intensive industry, such as a car industry, rather than in setting up a concern that requires a smaller amount of capital, such as a corner shop or a computer-programming office. New entrants would assess the extent of the 'barriers to entry', which may include: government regulations, distribution channels and location. The threat of new entrants is fairly low for industries such as car manufacturing and newspaper publishing but rather higher for a local shop.

4. **The bargaining power of suppliers** depends on the availability of substitute suppliers. As a sole supplier can have great power, it is unwise for any organisation to depend on a sole supplier; a sole supplier can quite easily raise prices or reduce quality with little risk to the retention of its customer organisations. Alternatively, where a particular organisation is the dominant customer of a supplier, that customer organisation is then in a relatively strong position, enabling it to demand lower prices, higher quality and better credit arrangements. Many retail chain stores hold strong customer power over suppliers, while established multinational suppliers, such as Microsoft, hold strong bargaining power over rival suppliers.

5. **The bargaining power of customers** increases as customer information and advertising inform customers about the full range of price and product options available. Customers can exert pressure on organisations by demanding lower prices or higher quality. Customers have more power where they make large purchases and where alternatives can easily be found. Organisations are in a weak position if they depend on a few large customers as these customer organisations may decide to switch to competing suppliers.

Porter suggested that an organisation could find competitive advantage against these competitive forces through pursuing one of three **generic strategies** (see Table 2.1). Each strategy imposes different pressures on an organisation attempting to ensure that resources and capabilities are consistent with the requirements of the strategy selected. The actual choice of generic strategy depends on:

- the fit between the demands of the strategy and an organisation's capabilities and resources
- the abilities of main competitors
- the key criteria for success in a market and their match with an organisation's capabilities.

The three alternative generic strategies are:
- differentiation strategies
- cost-leadership strategies
- focus strategies.

Strategy	*Features*	*Examples*
DIFFERENTIATION	Distinguishes products or services from competitors through superior quality. Customers must value the benefits more than the extra money they have to pay.	Gourmet restaurants, designer clothing
COST-LEADERSHIP	Operating more efficiently than competitors, thereby charging lower prices. Customers must be sensitive to price, but quality must be acceptable.	Supermarkets, discount shops
FOCUS	Concentrates on a specific group of buyers, usually aimed at a limited target segment.	Boat builders, antique dealers

Table 2.1 Porter's three generic strategies

1. The **differentiation strategy** involves an attempt to distinguish an organisation's products and services from others in the same industry segment. In order to succeed, an organisation must offer something to the customer that the customer values and which is different from the products or services of competing organisations. Product differentiation may involve branding, adding distinct features or providing extra services. If customers believe that a product is different from competitor products they may be prepared to pay higher prices. The value added, however, must be sufficient to command a premium price for the organisation to justify the *price–value relationship*. Chanel and Rolex are examples of organisations pursuing differentiation strategies within their respective market segments.

2. Through the **cost-leadership strategy**, an organisation seeks a cost advantage over its competitors. This involves reducing costs in order to undercut competitor prices while providing a product of a similar quality. The low price acts as a barrier against new entrants and substitute products.

3. A **focus strategy** is chosen by an organisation when it wants to be deliberately selective, focusing on a narrow group of customers, rather than on the whole market. The philosophy of a focus strategy is to specialise, thus meeting the needs of a clearly defined group far better than competing organisations would. Focus in itself might not be enough, however, and an organisation may have to combine it with cost-leadership or differentiation to build competitive advantage. Focus strategies are used, for example, by Internet web designers, beauticians and musicians.

Porter (1996) argued that choosing a unique position in industry is not enough to guarantee a sustainable competitive advantage, because a valuable position will attract imitating competitors. Porter believed that a manager's role is to create a fit among an organisation's activities and to integrate them so that an organisation does many things well. This requires trade-offs in competing in order to achieve a sustainable advantage, and therefore managers have to decide what *not* to do, as well as on what to do.

Some managers view their organisational environment as an 'uncontrollable' element, to which they must adapt. They passively accept the environment and do not try to change it. They analyse environmental forces and design strategies that should help the organisation avoid threats and take advantage of opportunities provided by the environment.

Other managers take an **environmental management perspective**, which means that, rather than simply watching and reacting, their organisations take aggressive actions to modify environmental forces. Organisations, for example, hire lobbyists to influence legislation affecting their industries and stage media events to gain favourable press coverage. But managers cannot always influence environmental forces; for example, it is difficult to influence geographical population shifts or the larger economic environment. Whenever possible, however, these managers take a proactive rather than reactive approach to their environment.

2.6 Key points

The *external environment* of an organisation is composed of non-specific elements within its surroundings with which it interacts and which affect its activities. These elements include:

- social aspects
- technological aspects
- economic aspects
- political–legal aspects.

The *internal* or *task environment* is composed of specific elements of an organisation's surroundings which affect its activities. These elements include:

- customers
- competitors
- suppliers
- distributors
- investors
- trade unions.

The *international dimension* is also an important element of the environment of management. The level of international business has increased in recent years. Managers need to have a clear understanding of the additional difficulties of managing internationally.

Porter suggested that an organisation's competitive environment is determined by 'five forces'. These are the:

- threat of new entrants
- bargaining power of suppliers
- bargaining power of buyers
- threat of substitute products
- rivalry among competitors.

The challenge for organisations is to achieve a competitive advantage and subsequently to sustain the advantage.

Porter also suggested that an organisation may gain its *competitive advantage* by pursuing one of three 'generic strategies'. These include:

- differentiation
- cost-leadership
- focus.

Organisations are affected by their external environment in several ways, for example, changing cultural values, competitive forces and uncertainty. Organisations use the elements of their internal environment to adapt to changes around them. The challenge for managers is to deal effectively with the constantly changing organisational environment in which they operate.

Important terms and concepts

bargaining power of customers (p.36)
bargaining power of suppliers (p.36)
competitive advantage (p.34)
competitive environment (p.34)
competitive rivalry (p.35)
competitors (p.31)
cost-leadership strategy (p.38)
cultural factors (p.27)
customers (p.30)
demographic factors (p.27)
differentiation strategy (p.37)
distributors (p.31)
economic environment (p.28)
external environment (p.26)
focus strategy (p.38)
geographic factors (p.27)
internal (task) environment (p.29)
international environment (p.33)
investors (p.32)
political–legal environment (p.29)
Porter's five forces (p.35)
social environment (p.26)
suppliers (p.31)
sustained competitive advantage (p.34)
technological environment (p.28)
threat of new entrants (p.36)
threat of substitutes (p.35)
three generic strategies (p.37)
trade unions (p.32)

Questions for review

1. List the forces in an organisation's external environment and discuss the impact these forces have on organisations. Illustrate your answer in the context of a real organisation.

2. List the forces in an organisation's internal environment and discuss the impact these forces have on organisations. Illustrate your answer in the context of a real organisation.

3. Explain:
   a. Competitive advantage
   b. Sustained competitive advantage.

   Illustrate your answers with examples from real organisations.

4. Choose an industry with which you are familiar and show how Porter's five forces affect that industry.

5. Discuss the advantages and disadvantages of each of the three generic strategies for an industry of your choice.

3
PLANNING AND DECISION-MAKING

Objectives

This chapter will help you to:

- understand the role of planning in management
- identify individual and organisational barriers to planning
- understand the role of decision-making in management
- identify models of decision-making.

3.1 Planning defined

> A plan is an explicit statement of intention that identifies both objectives and the actions needed to achieve them.

It is clear from Naylor's (2004) definition that a plan contains objectives and actions. The corporate objectives of an organisation emphasise its direct aims, which must be capable of measurement in order to confirm whether or not objectives are achieved. Organisational goals and aims are objectives that are restated in an operational and measurable form. When organisational objectives are combined with goals and aims they provide direction for an organisation. It is important that objectives are clearly expressed, realistic and have a deadline for completion.

Table 3.1 highlights the criteria for successful objectives, using the SMART acronym.

S	*Specific*: clearly and precisely expressed
M	*Measurable*: in order to ascertain whether or not they are achieved
A	*Agreed*: with those responsible for achieving them
R	*Realistic*: so that they can be achieved
T	*Timed*: with a deadline for achievement

Table 3.1 SMART objectives

The **action** part of the planning process clarifies the tasks required to achieve the objectives, and identifies those who are to carry out the tasks and when the actions are to be carried out. One of the major purposes of planning is to co-ordinate decision-making so that an organisation can move in a well-focused direction. Without planning the efforts of an organisation may not be well co-ordinated and managers and employees may be heading in different directions.

Planning is also closely linked with the control function of management. Planning, for example, sets the direction for the organisation, while control ensures that the direction is maintained or, if that proves impossible, it warns of the need to choose a new direction. The stages in the planning process are:

- formulate plans
- carry out plans
- compare outcomes with plans
- take corrective action (if necessary).

3.2 Levels of planning

Planning is undertaken by all managers in an organisation and is one of the core functions performed by managers. Three main levels of planning can be identified in organisations:

- strategic planning
- tactical planning
- operational planning.

Strategic plans are general plans outlining decisions regarding the allocation of resources, the priorities of an organisation and the course of action required to achieve strategic goals. These plans are set by the board of directors and top management; generally have an extended time horizon; and address questions of scope, resource deployment and competitive advantage.

Tactical plans are developed in order to implement specific parts of a strategic plan. Tactical plans specify both the resources and time available for specific projects, and generally flow from, and must be consistent with, a strategic plan. Tactical plans typically involve upper and middle management and, compared with strategic plans, have a somewhat shorter time horizon but with a more specific and concrete focus. Tactical plans, therefore, are concerned more with actually getting things done than with deciding what to do.

Operational plans focus on carrying out tactical plans in order to achieve operational goals. Operational plans are concerned with turning priorities into reality and are linked to physical and human resources. They may show how many people are to be involved with a particular project, as well as the skills and qualifications of the people involved. Table 3.2 details these three planning levels. Operational plans are developed by middle- and lower-level managers; operational plans have a short-term focus and are relatively narrow in scope.

Planning level	*Purpose*	*Performed by*	*Length of time*
STRATEGIC	• To establish organisational objectives and goals. • To match corporate objectives with available resources. • To assess external environment. • To assess internal environment.	Top managers (including, chief executive officers)	Long-range (for example, 3–5 years)
TACTICAL	• To implement specific parts of a strategic plan. • To give direction and allocate resources among sub-units or departments. • To focus on achievement, rather than deciding what to do.	Middle managers (for example, heads of departments)	Intermediate (for example, 1–5 years)
OPERATIONAL	• To focus on carrying out tactical plans. • To accomplish tasks with available resources. • To contribute to departmental objectives.	Supervisors (for example, office managers)	Short-range (for example, up to 1 year)

Table 3.2 Levels of planning in an organisation

The planning process attempts to guide an organisation from its current position to where it would like to be. Effective planning is based on the co-ordination and linking of plans between the three planning levels outlined above. Most organisations use all three levels of planning to guide future actions, though another important element of planning is the development of contingency plans.

Contingency planning is the development of an alternative course of action to be taken if a plan is unexpectedly disrupted or becomes inappropriate. A contingency plan is a plan devised for a specific situation when things could go wrong. Contingency plans are often devised by governments or businesses who want to be prepared for anything that could happen. They are sometimes known as 'back-up plans', 'worst-case scenario plans', or 'plan B'. Contingency plans are efforts to cater for the 'what if' questions that emerge in dynamic environments, such as the action to be taken if a major new competitor enters the same industry sector or if there is a supply shortage. In such cases previously made plans can be affected, and revised plans will be contingent on altered circumstances. Management, therefore, should always think through a number of options and their implications before a crisis arises. Contingency planning can be a 'rainy day plan', for example, used by organisers of outdoor events who plan alternative indoor activities in case of adverse weather conditions.

Contingency planning is becoming increasingly important for most organisations and especially for those operating in particularly complex or dynamic environments. Few managers have such an accurate view of the future that they can anticipate and plan for everything. Contingency planning is a useful technique for helping managers to cope with uncertainty and change.

3.3 Organisational goals

Organisations establish different kinds and levels of goals that determine organisational plans. Goals are critical to organisational effectiveness and they serve a number of purposes in the planning process. Goals, generally, have four purposes:

- providing guidance and a unified direction for people in the organisation
- goal-setting practices strongly affect other aspects of planning, for example, setting goals and developing plans to reach them are complementary activities
- serving as a source of motivation to employees
- providing an effective mechanism for evaluation and control.

Goals help to shape the various levels of organisational plans discussed above. According to Griffin (2008), there are generally four levels of goals in organisations:

- mission
- strategic goals
- tactical goals
- operational goals.

The **mission** or purpose is the organisation's reason for being. Pearce and David (1987) define an organisation's mission as:

> a statement of its fundamental, unique purpose that sets a business apart from other firms of its type and identifies the scope of the business's operations in product and market terms.

The mission is the foundation for all subsequent plans in an organisation. A **mission statement** is a statement of an organisation's purpose. Mission statements are widely seen as necessary in helping a company form its identity, purpose and direction. They are important instruments by which an organisation's essential values are conveyed to its stakeholders. Mission statements vary in length, complexity, detail and philosophy. Most mission statements tend to be generalised, but they provide a sense of direction to guide more detailed planning and strategy formulation. Mission statements usually contain vision (the desired future of an organisation) and strategic intentions (main activities, the desired position, and the support and constraints in achieving these activities). For example, the Dell computer company's mission statement proclaims that Dell aims to be 'the most successful computer company in the world at delivering the best customer experience in the markets we serve' (www.dell.com). In doing so, Dell aims to meet customer expectations in terms of:

- highest quality
- leading technology
- competitive pricing
- individual and company accountability
- best in class service and support
- flexible customisation capability
- superior corporate citizenship
- financial stability.

Other examples of mission statements include:

eBay: 'To provide a global trading platform where practically anyone can trade practically anything.' (www.ebay.com)

Facebook: 'To give people the power to share and make the world more open and connected.' (www.facebook.com)

Google: 'To organise the world's information and make it universally accessible and useful.' (www.google.com)

Amazon: 'To build a place where people can come to find and discover anything they might want to buy online.' (www.amazon.com)

Successful organisations operate according to their mission statements by ensuring that employees are aware of the mission statement in order to implement it. Mission statements, objectives and goals bring many benefits, including:

- *Unity of direction* — aiming for a co-ordinating effort (rather than individual efforts) by employees in achieving organisational objectives and goals
- *Motivation* — offering individuals a sense of personal achievement in the process of achieving objectives and committing them to their organisation
- *Basis of control* — providing criteria for measuring desired and actual outcomes from objectives denoting the performance that is expected of employees.

Strategic goals are set by organisations' top management (for example, the board of directors, chief executive officers, managing directors). These goals focus on broad issues and have a long-term time frame, typically three to five years.

Tactical goals are set by middle management. These goals focus on the actions necessary to achieve the broader strategic goals and have a medium-term time frame of one to five years.

Operational goals are set by lower-level managers. These goals focus on issues associated with tactical goals and have a short-term time frame, usually less than one year, but they can run for just weeks or days.

3.4 Barriers to planning

Planning can be obstructed by both individual and organisational barriers. **Individual barriers** to planning include:

- managers who believe that planning is unnecessary or a waste of time
- managers who may be more concerned with solving day-to-day matters rather than planning for the future
- managers who view planning as a threat
- managers who do not wish to commit themselves to specific planning objectives
- resistance to change (generally part of planning), because of fear of the unknown by managers and employees
- lack of clarity on the purpose of the planning process for employees who have been promoted to operational managerial positions and who have not received adequate training in planning.

Organisational barriers to planning include:

- inadequate support for planning from top management
- plans which may be too abstract to be translated into operational plans
- a dynamic and complex environment resulting in rapid change, which

militates against the proper assessment of future long-term opportunities and threats (for example, because of rapidly changing technological environments)

- an excessive emphasis on planning, leading to well-produced but over-sophisticated plans which may not be easy to implement.

Overcoming barriers to planning

1. **Understanding the purpose of plans**. Managers should recognise the basic purpose of planning and understand that well-executed plans will lead to more effective and efficient organisations.

2. **Communication and consultation**. Plans must be communicated to all employees in an organisation through proper communication channels (rather than through the grapevine or gossip). Managers and employees responsible for achieving organisational goals should be consulted to ensure a sense of 'ownership' of the plans.

3. **Training**. Appropriate training in planning skills will reduce insecurity and uncertainty and help plans to be implemented effectively.

4. **Top management support**. Top managers need to be actively involved and educated to see the benefits of planning in order to help middle-level and lower-level managers recognise top management's view of planning as an important managerial function.

5. **Developing plans with clear objectives and goals**. Plans should not be conceived to be too abstract, but should have easily identifiable targets which all employees should readily understand.

3.5 Planning in practice: management by objectives

In 1954, Peter Drucker first proposed **management by objectives (MBO)** as a method of implementing strategic objectives. MBO attempts to integrate individual and organisational objectives. With this, the responsibilities of each employee are specified in terms of measurable results so that they can be used by employees in planning work. The MBO philosophy promotes employee participation when setting objectives as this strengthens the motivation to achieve the objectives. The results can be monitored by employees as well as managers. MBO provides a method of involving all employees and focusing individual objectives to be integrated in a strategic plan.

A primary step in MBO is the communication, by managers to employees, of organisational goals and plans that have been established. Goals are then specified for accomplishment in particular time frames. Plans developed to achieve particular goals are stated clearly and linked directly to each goal. In order to facilitate the achievement of both personal and organisational goals and plans, managers, in conjunction with employees, must first ensure that the goals that are set *are* attainable.

MBO allows the review and adjustment of previously set objectives in order for them to remain relevant and achievable, and feedback can be used for employees' personal development and be built into employee performance appraisal, which is conducted regularly (often annually) by many organisations. The advantages of MBO are recognised in terms of individual improvements on past performance, particularly where individual employees determine their own objectives and where there is feedback on performance.

3.6 Decision-making

Decision-making is the act of choosing from among alternatives. Decision-making means choosing one option from a number of options, that is, options have to be identified and the 'best' option chosen. The decision-making process, therefore, includes recognising and defining the nature of a decision situation, identifying alternatives, selecting the 'best' choice and putting it into practice. The word 'best' implies effectiveness. Effective decision-making requires the decision-maker to understand the situation driving the decision. Decision-making is closely linked to the planning process because managers developing and implementing plans, at all levels, have to make decisions on organisational strategies. Decisions can be divided into three main categories:

- strategic
- administrative
- operational.

Strategic decisions are concerned with the achievement of long-term corporate plans and organisational objectives. Strategic decisions are usually big, risky and hard to reverse with significant long-term effects. They can be a major source of organisational learning and they play an important role in the development of individual managers. These decisions are made by top management, often made after lengthy consideration of all related factors, because the decisions may have major consequences for the future of an organisation. Strategic decisions could include, for example:

- the introduction of a new product
- how to deal with international competition
- forming strategic alliances

and many other significant options. Strategic decisions are typically related to one-off (rather than ongoing or routine) situations where each individual situation is considered and evaluated as it arises.

Administrative decisions follow from strategic decisions and are concerned with establishing ways to implement procedures and systems so that an organisation can operate in an effective and efficient manner. Administrative decisions also support operational decisions (see below). Examples of administrative decisions include procedures governing:

- payroll
- contracting of suppliers and distributors
- decisions on human resource procedures.

Though they are relatively infrequently required, administrative decisions are usually made by middle managers.

Operational decisions are day-to-day procedural decisions that have to be made on an ongoing basis. Operational decisions are made by front-line managers (or supervisors) and operate in the short term. Examples of operational decisions include:

- reordering office supplies
- calculating holiday pay
- dealing with more routine demands
- customer complaints.

Managers making operational decisions are helped by procedures that have previously been put in place, for example, standard guidelines for reordering supplies or for dealing with complaints made by customers.

3.7 Models of decision-making

Two well-recognised models of decision-making are the *classical* model and the *administrative* model.

The **classical model** guides managers on how they should make decisions. The classical model emphasises the making of decisions in a rational and logical manner, and presumes that:

- decision-makers seek full information on practically all options before making a choice
- objectives are clear and agreed

- problems are clearly defined
- decision-makers can eliminate situations of uncertainty to achieve a condition of certainty for any decision
- decision-makers evaluate all aspects of a decision situation logically and rationally.

There are, however, some problems associated with the classical model and, indeed, management theorists have concluded that managers are often unable to make rational decisions because of the following:

- The classical model sets out how decisions should be made, but does not describe how managers make decisions in practice.
- Problems are usually ill-defined.
- Objectives are often unclear.
- It is almost impossible to consider *all* other options.
- Very few conditions of real certainty exist.
- Decision-makers may not evaluate all situations rationally and logically but may be influenced by political, social and cultural norms.
- Decision-makers may make decisions based merely on intuition or on a hunch, therefore not making the 'logical' decision that the classical model requires.

Herbert A. Simon recognised that decisions are not always made with rationality and logic, and his **administrative model** describes his view of how decisions are often *actually* made, in contrast to prescribing how decisions *should* be made. The administrative model recognises that:

- objectives are often unclear and may not have been agreed
- problems may not have been clearly specified
- decision-makers' searches for options are limited
- decision criteria may not have been established in advance.

Decision-makers, faced with these problems, often:

- have incomplete and imperfect information on which to base their decisions
- are constrained by *bounded rationality*
- tend to *satisfice* when making decisions.

Bounded rationality means that people set limits on how rational they can be. The boundary may arise from previous experiences of decision-making, skills and habits.

Satisficing means choosing the first option that meets the minimum decision criteria rather than conducting an exhaustive search for the best possible option. Decision-makers tend to satisfice because of the problems associated with collecting, memorising, comprehending and communicating vast amounts of information.

In summary, the classical model is prescriptive as it explains how decision-makers might attempt to be more rational and logical in their approach to decisions. On the other hand, the administrative model can be used by decision-makers to develop a better understanding of the limitations in the decision-making process. Two other important decision processes are **intuition** and **escalation of commitment**.

Intuition, as previously mentioned, is a belief about something without conscious consideration. Managers sometimes make decisions because it 'feels right' or they have a hunch. This feeling is often based on years of experience and practice in making decisions in similar situations. Managers should be careful, however, not to rely on intuition too heavily.

Escalation of commitment occurs when a decision-maker stays with a decision even when it appears to be wrong. Decision-makers sometimes make decisions and then become so committed to the course of action suggested by that decision that they stay with it.

3.8 The decision-making process

In attempting to make good decisions, managers generally go through various procedural steps (outlined in Figure 3.1).

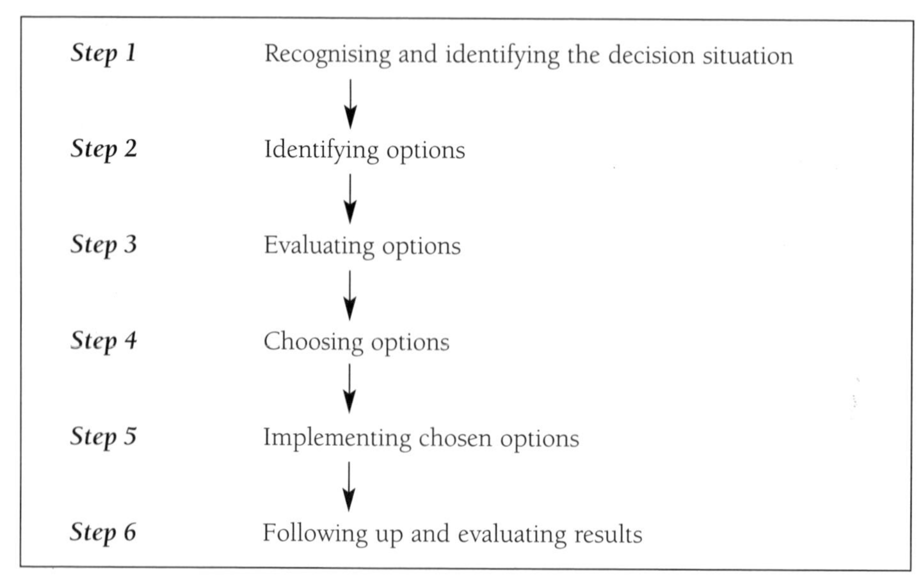

Figure 3.1 The decision-making process

Just as different types of decisions can be made, varying conditions exist in which managers have to make decisions:

- *Certainty* — where managers make decisions in circumstances of certainty, the available options and conditions associated with each option are known to be certain. Very few decisions, however, are made with certainty because of the turbulent environment in which organisations operate.
- *Risk* — where managers make decisions under risk, the available options are known, but their outcomes are doubtful.
- *Uncertainty* — where managers make decisions with uncertainty, only some of the available options and their associated risks are known.
- *Recognising and identifying the decision situation* — acknowledging the reason for a decision; the reason may be positive or negative. In many negative situations there are no prior warnings, for example, in the case of mechanical failure. Once the decision recognition phase has occurred, a manager has to ensure that a clear definition of the opportunity or problem is provided.
- *Identifying options* — managers should try to identify as many options as possible in order to reach the 'best' decision. Managers may be constrained by financial, legal, economic and political forces in identifying options.
- *Evaluating options* — having identified a number of options, managers can evaluate each identified option. Options are evaluated on a number of criteria, such as, feasibility, projected satisfactory outcome, financial implications and the manner in which each option fits with overall organisational objectives.
- *Implementing chosen options* — after an option has been decided on, it can be implemented. The successful implementation of any option usually requires managers to communicate the basis for their decision to employees, so that employees can understand the decision and give their commitment to implementing the particular option chosen.
- *Following up and evaluating results* — after the decision has been implemented, managers need to evaluate the results and provide feedback to employees. Evaluation helps managers assess whether the decision has been effective, and also helps with future decision-making.

3.9 Group decision-making

In many organisations decisions are made by groups and teams, rather than by individuals. One example of this is **brainstorming**. When brainstorming, group members are encouraged to generate as many ideas about a particular topic as they can. For instance, group members may use brainstorming to generate as many solutions as they can and group members should be encouraged to say anything that comes to mind when brainstorming. Every idea is written down and judgments about ideas are saved until later, when the group returns to all of the ideas and selects those that are most useful. In some situations groups will provide the best decisions and in other situations individuals will be better. Table 3.3 summarises the advantages and disadvantages of group decision-making.

Advantages	*Disadvantages*
More information and knowledge become available.	Group decisions take longer and increase costs.
The number of possible options is likely to be increased.	Groups can be indecisive and may satisfice rather than seeking all the available options.
The involvement of more people should increase the likelihood of acceptance of the decision.	Groups may be dominated by an individual with a strong personality.
Better communication of a decision should result.	Groupthink may occur (where a group wishes to reach a decision without reaching the best possible decision).

Table 3.3 Advantages and disadvantages of group decision-making

3.10 Key points

The *planning process* is an essential managerial function for organisations, where managers develop different types of goals and plans. To serve a variety of purposes, organisations develop various goals, for example:

- mission
- strategic goals
- tactical goals
- operational goals.

Organisational goals help managers develop organisational plans. The main types of plan are:

- *Strategic* — set by top management, addressing long-term issues for an entire organisation

- *Tactical* — in operation at the middle level of an organisation, developed in order to implement specific parts of a strategic plan, having an intermediate time frame
- *Operational* — implemented at the lower level of an organisation, with a short time frame, aimed at achieving operational goals.

Individual and organisational barriers to planning may exist despite the benefits of planning, which should be obvious to managers. Managers have to develop a number of strategies to successfully overcome these barriers. An example of planning in practice is MBO, which attempts to integrate individual and organisational objectives in an overall strategic plan.

Decisions, even if usually associated with the planning process, are a core part of all managerial activities. *Decision-making* is the act of choosing one option from a number of options. Decisions are made under conditions of certainty, risk or uncertainty. Decisions can be made by individuals or groups, with either option having both advantages and disadvantages. Two recognised models of decision-making are the classical model and the administrative model.

The *classical model* assumes that managers have complete information and that they will behave rationally.

The *administrative model* recognises that managers do not always have complete information, that they may not always act rationally and that they may satisfice.

Important terms and concepts

Questions for review

1. Explain the purposes of planning in an organisation.

2. Describe the barriers to effective planning and suggest how these barriers might be overcome.

3. Distinguish between strategic, tactical, operational and contingency planning.

4. Describe the steps in the decision-making process. Illustrate each step with an example.

5. Distinguish between strategic, administrative and operational decisions.

6. Compare and contrast the classical and administrative models of decision-making.

4
LEADING AND LEADERSHIP

Objectives

This chapter will help you to:
- describe leadership
- trace the development of leadership theories
- understand different theories of leadership
- identify the relationship between leadership styles and management.

4.1 Leadership defined

> Leadership is the process of motivating people to act in particular ways in order to achieve specific goals.

Naylor's (2004) definition indicates clearly that leadership is an ongoing process which involves the motivation of others to achieve the common goals of an organisation. Authority and responsibility are essential components of leadership in deciding the way forward and in the success or failure of achieving agreed goals. Leadership provides inspiration and guidance through interaction with others to achieve certain ends. It also involves **power**, which is usually defined as *the potential to influence the behaviour of others*. According to Hannagan (2008), if leadership is seen as a process and as a series of actions which can be identified, then it can be learned, to some extent.

In recent years, the word 'vision' has become more closely associated with leaders and leadership. Vision, in essence, is what an organisation wants to become. A vision communicates both the purpose and values of an organisation (values are guiding beliefs about how things should be done).

4.2 Theories of leadership

Leadership has been a subject of investigation for centuries, but it is only from the 1950s onwards that theories of leadership have emerged. Various theories have been put forward, from the traditional view that leaders are born, not made, to the more recent view that leadership depends on particular situations rather than on a particular set of universally shared traits. In an effort to recognise the 'exceptional characteristics' that leaders possess, one of the earliest theories of leadership concentrated on identifying leadership traits.

Trait theories

The scientific study of leadership began with a focus on the traits of effective leaders. Leader trait research examined the physical, mental and social characteristics of individuals.

Trait theories concentrated on the *qualities* required for effective leaders, suggesting that leaders are born and not made. Trait theorists sought to identify those traits which were common to all leaders and which caused them to be self-selected leaders. The traits or characteristics that appeared most frequently were:

- intelligence
- height (that is, physically tall)
- energy
- initiative
- maturity
- vision.

Despite various studies of leadership, however, no common characteristics have emerged. Research has found that particular traits or characteristics, that separate leaders from non-leaders, cannot be identified — contrary to the view that leaders are born and not made. It is now recognised that certain traits increase the likelihood that a leader will be effective, but they do not guarantee effectiveness, and the relative importance of different traits is dependent upon the nature of the leadership situation.

Leader behaviour approach

Partially as a result of the disillusionment with the trait approach to leadership that occurred by the beginning of the 1950s, the focus of leadership research shifted away from leader traits to leader behaviours. The premise of this stream of research was that the behaviours exhibited by leaders are more important than their physical, mental or emotional traits. The two most famous behavioural leadership studies took place at the University of Michigan and Ohio State University in the late 1940s and 1950s.

Michigan studies

Researchers at the University of Michigan, USA, studied leadership during the 1940s and reported their findings in 1950. These studies were based on interviews with leaders (managers) and followers (employees). Led by Rensis Likert, the results of the interviews produced the **Michigan continuum**, which suggests that leaders are either people-focused or task-focused (Figure 4.1).

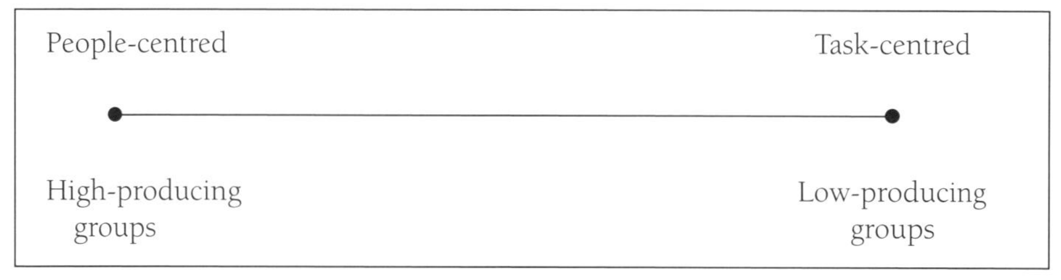

Figure 4.1 The Michigan continuum

People-focused managers:
- pay close attention to the work relationships of their employees
- encourage employee participation in decision-making
- strive for job satisfaction for their employees.

Task-focused managers, at the other end of the continuum:
- pay close attention to explaining work procedures clearly
- are more directive
- are interested in performance.

Likert argued that people-focused leaders tend to be more effective, as his studies showed that managers who are people-focused are high-producing leaders. Managers who are task-focused tend to be less productive. The Michigan studies also found that people-focused leader behaviour tended to be organic and flexible, whereas task-focused leader behaviour tended to be rigid and bureaucratic. Leaders, however, may have a style which lies somewhere in between and it should be noted that Likert studied only the two end styles for contrast.

Ohio State studies

During the late 1940s, researchers at Ohio State University in the USA also identified two styles of leadership. Their studies were based on extensive questionnaire surveys and produced results similar to the findings of the

Michigan studies. The terms used by the researchers at Ohio State University were *consideration* and *initiating structure*.

Consideration leadership has an *informal* approach to management which:

- considers employees' feelings
- focuses on employees' well-being
- provides feedback to employees
- encourages the participation of all employees through two-way dialogue and communication
- promotes a 'good' working environment for managers and employees.

This behaviour involves a leader's concern for improving communication and developing mutual trust and liking between the leader and employees. The Ohio State studies viewed **consideration** as behaviour indicative of friendship, mutual trust, respect and warmth in the relationship between the leader and the members of his or her staff.

The **initiating-structure** leadership style defines clearly who the leader is and has a *formal* management approach and focuses on issues such as:

- planning
- organising
- controlling
- allocating tasks
- work processes in general.

Initiating structure involves a leader clearly indicating the relationship between himself or herself and members of the organisation, and endeavouring to establish well-defined channels of communication and methods of procedures throughout the organisation.

The major difference between the Ohio State studies and the Michigan studies is that the Ohio researchers believed that it was possible for leaders to practise both consideration *and* initiating-structure styles of leadership. The Ohio State researchers, for example, showed that it was possible for a manager to score high on consideration and also on initiating-structure.

In summary, leadership which is high on both initiating structure and consideration behaviours tends to be the most effective form of leadership.

Leadership grid

An extension of the Ohio State studies was the *leadership* or *management grid*.

The **leadership grid** (Figure 4.2) provides a means of evaluating leadership styles and was introduced by Blake and Mouton in 1962 and suggests that leadership behaviour is multidimensional insofar as leaders can exhibit a number of behaviours that interact with each other. Blake and Mouton suggested 81 possible interactions, but defining each of these positions was not practical, so five extreme positions were described. The horizontal axis represents *concern for production* (similar to task-centred and initiating-structure behaviour) and the vertical axis represents *concern for people* (similar to employee-centred and consideration behaviour).

Blake and Mouton defined *concern for production* as concern with whatever an organisation seeks to achieve. *Concern for people* refers to a leader's attention to the people who are engaged with achieving organisational goals. This concern includes building organisational commitment and trust, promoting personal worth of employees, providing proper working conditions and rewards, and promoting good interpersonal relations.

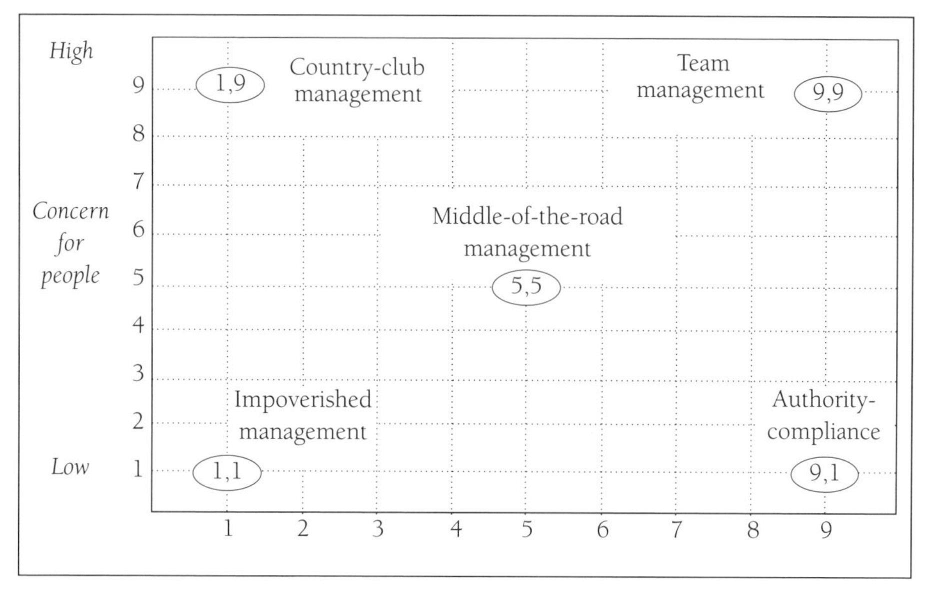

Figure 4.2 Blake and Mouton's leadership/management grid

Source: Blake, R. and J. Mouton. 1962. 'The Managerial Grid', *Advanced Managerial Office Executive*, Vol. 1, no.9.

The five positions identified in the grid are:

- *Impoverished management* — score 1,1 on the grid — low concern for both employees and production. Managers operating an impoverished management style avoid responsibility and contact with employees, and rely on previous practice to run an organisation.
- *Authoritarian management* — score 9,1 on the grid — high levels of concern for production and efficiency and low levels of concern for employees. As this management style is task-oriented, managers believe

that their responsibility is to plan, direct and control their employees. Authoritarian managers also believe that employees are a commodity just like machines and enforce their own decisions over the wishes of their employees.

- *Middle-of-the-road management* — score 5,5 on the grid — unlikely to involve managers who are dynamic leaders. Middle-of-the-road managers believe in compromise, whereby they get acceptable levels of production but also have concern for employees. These managers have confidence in their employees and make decisions only when endorsed by their employees.
- *Country-club management* — score 1,9 on the grid — high emphasis on concern for people and low emphasis on concern for production. Employees working with this style of leadership report high levels of satisfaction as they are encouraged and supported by their managers, and employees tend to work in harmony.
- *Team management* — score 9,9 on the grid — high on concern for both employees and production. Managers operating the team management style believe that concern for employees and tasks are compatible. These managers aim at combining the highest possible standard of production with all employees agreeing on a high level of commitment in order to achieve the best possible results for all stakeholders. Blake and Mouton argued that this management style provides the most effective leadership as it fosters long-term development and teamwork.

Contingency (situational) approaches to leadership

Contingency approaches to leadership assume that appropriate leader behaviour depends on situational variables. Different situations demand different kinds of leadership, requiring individual leaders to adapt styles to the requirements of different situations.

Tannenbaum and Schmidt's contingency theory

Research on effective leadership styles have shown that these depend on many variables, such as:

- management style
- individual personality
- the culture in the organisation
- the tasks to be performed.

The contingency approach suggests that there is no leadership style that is effective in all situations. In 1958, Robert Tannenbaum and Warner Schmidt developed a **leadership continuum** (see Figure 4.3) which suggested that various factors influenced the choice of leadership styles. They concluded that there are three main factors or 'forces' from which a leadership style is developed:

- *Personal forces*, such as the personal background of managers, their confidence, and experience
- *Characteristics of subordinates*, such as a manager's need to consider the willingness or unwillingness of subordinates to accept responsibility and to make decisions
- *The situation itself*, which suggests that managers need to recognise the situation in which they find themselves, in the context of their corporate culture, colleagues' work style, and the time limit and nature of the tasks to be performed.

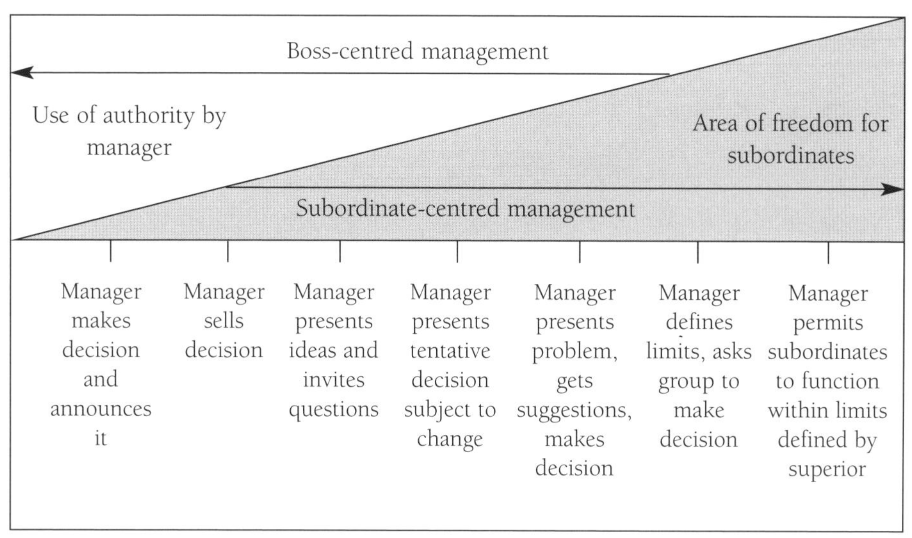

Figure 4.3 Tannenbaum and Schmidt's leadership continuum

Source: Tannenbaum, R. and W. Schmidt. 1958. 'How to Choose a Leadership Pattern', *Harvard Business Review*, March/April.

Common to all contingency approaches is the requirement for leaders to behave in a flexible manner, and to have the ability to diagnose and apply the leadership style appropriate to any particular situation.

The continuum identifies extremes in leadership styles: for example, at one end the autocratic leader (using what Tannenbaum and Schmidt term 'boss-centred leadership') who makes all decisions alone; at the other end employees having complete freedom to make decisions with minimal guidance (which they term 'subordinate-centred leadership'). Between these two extremes, according to Tannenbaum and Schmidt, there are a number of points on the continuum that influence leadership style and each point is influenced by the three forces identified (personal forces, characteristics of subordinate and the situation itself).

In suggesting that leaders might vary their styles, Tannenbaum and Schmidt viewed leadership as something that could be learned from experience. They challenged the belief that either directive (autocratic) or participative (democratic) leadership was superior. They contended, for example, that a directive leader was better when time was scarce or when circumstances were difficult, such as in a crisis situation. Alternatively, participative leadership was more appropriate where experienced subordinates could exercise good decision-making skills.

Overall, the leadership continuum suggests that leadership style shifts the focus from the individual manager in isolation to the manager in the context of the combined tasks to be performed and the characteristics of the subordinates.

Fiedler's contingency theory

Fiedler developed his **leadership contingency model** in 1967. This model suggests that the appropriate style of leadership varies with the favourableness of the situation. Fiedler believed that the performance of employees is contingent on a leader adopting an appropriate style, depending on the situation being favourable or unfavourable. Fiedler suggested that the three most important variables in determining the relative favourableness of a situation are:

- *Leader–member relations* — the relationship between a leader and employees in regard to issues such as trust, respect and confidence in each other. Good relations foster the effectiveness of a leader.
- *Degree of structure in task* — the defining of tasks for employees. A task is structured when it is routine, unambiguous and easily understood. An unstructured task is non-routine and complex. A structured task is more favourable for a leader as employees will know what to do, without major guidance from a leader.
- *Power and authority of the position* — if the leader has power and authority to act on each situation, power is assumed to be strong. Alternatively, if a leader has to seek approval from others, power is assumed to be weak. From the leader's point of view, the position of strong power and authority is more favourable.

From these three variables, Fiedler suggested that leaders are either *task-oriented* (similar to initiating-structure behaviour) or *relationship-oriented* (similar to people-focused or consideration behaviour). Fiedler suggested that the most favourable situation for leaders to influence their group was one in which they have good leader–member relations, hold high position power, and are directing a high task structure. In contrast, a most unfavourable situation for leaders is where they are disliked, have little position power and face an unstructured task. From questionnaires, Fiedler developed an instrument called the **least-preferred co-worker (LPC)** to classify these two leadership styles. The measuring scale asks leaders to describe people with whom they have worked and to think of the one with whom they worked least well. The leader is given a set of sixteen scales, and the leader's LPC is calculated by totalling the numbers marked on each scale. Figure 4.4 illustrates two of the sixteen scales.

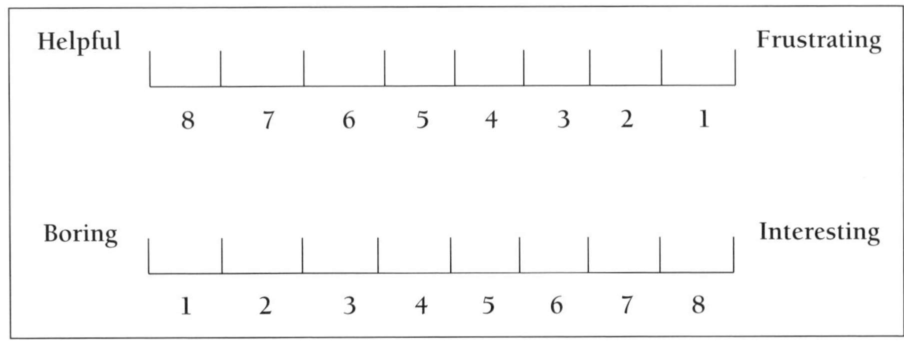

Figure 4.4 The least-preferred co-worker theory of leadership

Fiedler suggested that a high total score reflects a relationship-oriented leader, but that relationship-motivated leaders will score relationship issues high despite their problems with the LPC. A low score reflects a task-oriented leader, but rates the LPC low on all dimensions. Fiedler believed that both these leadership styles are effective, depending on the situation involved.

Fiedler suggested that task-motivated leaders have low LPC scores; they focus on details; and will be tough and autocratic on any uncommitted subordinates in order to complete a task. Their self-esteem comes from completing tasks. They are only considerate when tasks are going well. Productivity holds the higher value for these leaders. Relation-motivated leaders, have high LPC scores, get bored with details and focus instead on pleasing others, getting loyalty and being accepted. Their self-esteem comes from interpersonal relationships.

Vroom-Yetton-Jago contingency theory

Victor Vroom, Philip Yetton and Arthur Jago based their model of leadership style on the decision-making practices of managers. This model is narrower than other contingency theories insofar as it focuses on one part of the leadership process, that is, the amount of decision-making participation that, ideally, should be granted to employees. The model was first proposed by Vroom and Yetton in 1973 and was revised and expanded by Vroom and Jago in 1988. They suggested that decisions are generally characterised by three variables:

- the quality of the decision (the effect of the decision on performance)
- acceptance of the decision by employees (the extent to which employees are committed to the decision)
- the time needed for the decision to be made.

The Vroom-Yetton-Jago model outlines decision styles, which range from the purely autocratic (AI) at one end to total participation style (G) at the opposite end.

The Vroom-Yetton-Jago contingency theory suggests that, depending on these three variables, it is possible for leaders to select a decision style. Their theories proposed five main decision styles for leaders that depend on the degree of participation by employees in the decision-making process:

- *Autocratic I (AI)* — managers make the decisions themselves using available information.
- *Autocratic II (AII)* — managers obtain information from employees regarding the decisions to be made but make the decisions themselves.
- *Consultative I (CI)* — managers obtain and share information regarding decisions to be made with employees individually but the managers make the decisions themselves and these may or may not be influenced by the opinions of employees.
- *Consultative II (CII)* — managers share the decisions to be made with employees as a group and obtain their ideas and information, but the managers may or may not use the ideas generated when making decisions.
- *Group participation (G)* — managers share the decisions to be made with employees as a group, which allows for managers and employees to consider various solutions; managers act as co-ordinators in order to reach an agreement, which might then be implemented.

The Vroom-Yetton-Jago model suggests that leaders might choose between different styles depending on the particular decision-making circumstances. This contrasts with the views of Tannenbaum and Schmidt who believed that different leaders had different styles, but would consistently follow their own particular style.

Path-goal theory

The path-goal theory was proposed by Martin Evans and Robert House and is associated with the motivation of employees (see Chapter 7). The path-goal theory suggests that leaders can influence employees by recognising and satisfying their expectations. The theory also suggests that leaders can make valued or desired rewards available and ensure that employees understand the behaviour which should lead to those rewards. The path-goal theory suggests that leaders should motivate employees (through support, direction, guidance and training) and clarify the paths for employees to attain their goals. According to the path-goal theory there are two main variables which influence leadership style:

- Personal characteristics, which include factors such as:
  - ability
  - skills
  - motivation.
- Workplace characteristics, which include factors such as:
  - rules governing authority and responsibility
  - the clarity of a task to be executed.

Path-goal theory, therefore, is concerned with a leader clarifying the path and adjusting the goals to help employees accomplish their goals and receive valued rewards. The path-goal theory identifies four kinds of leader behaviour:

- *Directive leadership* — managers tell employees what they have to do, let employees know what is expected of them and give guidance and direction.
- *Supportive leadership* — managers adopt a friendly and approachable style, display concern for the welfare of employees and treat employees as equals.
- *Participative leadership* — managers consult employees, take their opinions into account and allow participation in decision-making.
- *Achievement-oriented leadership* — managers set clear and challenging goals, encourage employees and expect them to perform at high levels.

In summary, the path-goal theory assumes that managers can change leadership styles in order to meet the demands of particular situations. Personal characteristics and workplace characteristics are recognised as the two key variables that define the behaviour of leaders, and this in turn can influence the behaviour of employees.

From the above theories, it is clear that leadership is a social process that involves interaction with others. In a constantly changing social, economic, and technological environment, leadership has become more important than it was in the past.

In summary, an examination of recent leadership literature shows that prevailing leadership thinking is dominated by *contingency* theory. The contingency theory holds that leadership has to continually adapt in order to respond to ongoing changing contexts. As organisations are continually changing, this implies that leadership also has to continually change, since leadership has to respond to new and unique sets of circumstances on a daily basis.

Leadership styles

Kurt Lewin's leadership styles

In 1939, a group of researchers led by psychologist Kurt Lewin set out to identify different styles of leadership. While further research has identified more specific types of leadership, this early study was very influential and established three major leadership styles.

- *Authoritarian leadership (autocratic)* — Authoritarian leaders provide clear expectations for what needs to be done, when it should be done, and how it should be done. There is also a clear division between the leader and the followers. Authoritarian leaders make decisions independently with little or no input from the rest of the group. As all decision-making powers are centralised in the leader they, therefore, do not entertain any suggestions or initiatives from subordinates. Authoritarian leadership is best applied to situations where there is little time for group decision-making or where the leader is the most knowledgeable member of the group.
- *Participative leadership (democratic)* — Lewin's study found that participative (democratic) leadership is generally the most effective leadership style. The democratic leadership style favours decision-making by the group. Democratic leaders offer guidance to group members, but they also participate in the group and allow input from other group members. Participative leaders encourage group members to participate, but retain the final say over the decision-making process. Group members feel engaged in the process and are more motivated and creative.
- *Delegative (laissez-faire)* — Delegative leaders do not lead but allow maximum freedom to subordinates. They offer little or no guidance to group members and leave decision-making up to group members. While this style can be effective in situations where group members are highly qualified in an area of expertise, it often leads to poorly defined roles and a lack of motivation.

Transformational leadership

Transformational leadership is one of the most topical approaches in leadership studied since the early 1980s. Transformational leadership is a process that is meant to transform individuals. It assesses followers' motives, endeavours to satisfy their needs and respects their dignity as human beings. Transformational leaders are seen as visionaries who challenge people to achieve high standards in everything they do. Transformational leadership is a process that includes:

- charismatic leadership (sharing complete faith in a leader)
- inspirational motivation/leadership (communicating high performance expectations)
- intellectual stimulation (enabling others to think about old problems in new ways)
- individualised consideration (actively giving personal attention to all individuals).

Changes in the marketplace and workforce in the last quarter of the twentieth century have resulted in the need for leaders to become more transformational and less transactional, if they are to remain effective. **Transactional leadership** is viewed as manipulative, using continual bargaining to determine what employees need to do to achieve personal and organisational objectives. In contrast, **transformational leaders** motivate followers to achieve more than they would have expected by raising motivation and the importance of the value of individuals' tasks within an organisation. Transformational leaders go beyond transactional leadership by using the power of their own vision and energy in order to inspire their employees.

Servant leadership

This approach to leadership reflects a philosophy that leaders should be servants first. Servant leadership suggests that leaders must place the needs of subordinates, customers and the community ahead of their own interests in order to be effective. Characteristics of servant leaders include: empathy, stewardship, and commitment to the personal and professional growth of their subordinates. Servant leadership has not been subjected to extensive empirical testing but has generated considerable interest among both leadership scholars and practitioners.

Leadership versus management

Leadership should be distinguished from management. Management is broader in scope and involves planning, organising, staffing, directing and controlling, and a manager is someone who performs these functions. A manager has formal authority by virtue of his or her position or office. Leadership, by contrast, primarily deals with influence. A manager may or may not be an effective leader. Leaderships involves risk-taking and motivating and inspiring people to achieve goals. A leader's ability to influence others may be based on a variety of factors other than his or her formal authority or position. In summary, leadership determines *where* an organisation is going and influences people in particular directions, whereas management describes *how* the organisation can get there.

According to Senge (1990), 'leadership is a phenomenon, not a position'. It is not determined by hierarchy, as leaders can emerge from teams of middle management. Senge suggests that leaders are people who move ahead and who have some influence over others. Capowski (1994) suggests that management and leadership differ in that one comes from the head and the other from the heart. The manager is associated with qualities that come from the head:

- rationality
- tough-mindedness
- authority
- analysis
- structure
- persistence
- problem-solving
- stabilising.

The leader, on the other hand, is associated with qualities that come from the heart:

- creativeness
- flexibility
- inspiring others
- innovativeness
- courage
- imagination
- vision
- initiating change.

Kotter (1986) made a more detailed distinction. He saw management as predominantly *activity* based, whereas leadership means dealing with people rather than things. Currently there is a great deal of emphasis on developing leadership in those with responsibilities for managing people. Effective leadership has become one of the current management issues in organisations. There is a particular emphasis on transformational or visionary leadership and the ability to inspire others through instilling the purpose and mission of the organisation. Kotter (1990) also suggests that good managers produce orderly, predictable results; keep things on schedule and within budget; and make things work efficiently. Clearly, organisations benefit from good management. On the other hand, good leaders produce important, positive change by providing vision, aligning people's efforts with the organisation's direction, and keeping people focused on the mission and vision by motivating and inspiring them. Good leadership, like good management, helps an organisation to succeed.

In practice, however, the most effective managers are also leaders and the quality of leadership has become an increasingly important part of management ability. Organisations need both management and leadership in order to successfully achieve organisational goals.

MANAGEMENT PRODUCES ORDER AND CONSISTENCY	LEADERSHIP PRODUCES CHANGE AND MOVEMENT
• Planning and budgeting	• Establishing direction
• Establishing agendas	• Creating a vision
• Setting timetables	• Clarifying the big picture
• Allocating resources	• Setting strategies
• Organising and staffing	• Aligning people
• Providing structure	• Communicating goals
• Making job replacements	• Seeking commitment
• Establishing rules and procedures	• Building teams and coalitions
• Controlling and problem solving	• Motivating and inspiring
• Developing incentives	• Inspiring and energising
• Generating creative solutions	• Empowering subordinates
• Taking corrective action	• Satisfying unmet needs

Table 4.1 A comparison of management and leadership competencies

Source: Northouse 2007

4.3 Key points

Various theories of leadership (summarised in Table 4.2) have emerged during the past century.

The *trait approach* to leadership was one of the first studies conducted with the aim of identifying important leadership traits. The trait approach initially assumed that some common traits separated leaders from non-leaders. The results of the research, however, suggested that there were no traits common to all leaders.

Subsequent research at the University of Michigan and Ohio State University identified two basic forms of leadership behaviour: one concentrated on *work* and the *tasks* to be performed; the other focused on employee *welfare* and support for employees. Another approach to leadership is shown in the *leadership grid*, which identifies wide variations in leadership and management styles.

Theory	*Characteristics*
TRAIT THEORY	Attempted to identify traits common to all leaders.
MICHIGAN STUDIES	Leaders are either people- or task-focused.
OHIO STATE STUDIES	Leadership style uses either initiating-structure or consideration behaviour.
LEADERSHIP GRID	Leadership is multidimensional, a mix of concern for production and people.
TANNENBAUM AND SCHMIDT	Leadership continuum suggesting that leaders are either boss- or subordinate-centred.
FIEDLER	Style of leadership varies between task- and relationship orientation depending on the situation.
VROOM-YETTON-JAGO	Leadership style is based on the decision-making practices of managers.
PATH-GOAL THEORY	A leader's primary functions are to make desired rewards available to employees and to clarify for employees the behaviour that will lead to those rewards.
TRANSFORMATIONAL LEADERSHIP	Leaders are seen as visionaries who challenge people to achieve high standards in everything they do.
SERVANT LEADERSHIP	Leaders should be servants first.

Table 4.2 Summary of leadership theories

Contingency approaches to leadership recognise that the behaviour of leaders is not universally applicable to all situations; rather, a particular situation dictates the behaviour of leaders. Fiedler's leadership contingency model, for example, suggested that the style of leadership varies depending on a particular situation or context.

The *leadership continuum*, developed by Tannenbaum and Schmidt, suggests that leaders are at either end of a continuum, that is, they are either boss-centred or subordinate-centred. Similarly, the LPC (least-preferred co-worker) scale suggests that a leader's behaviour should be either task- or relationship-oriented, depending on the particular situation.

The *path-goal theory* suggests that a leader's behaviour may be supportive of employees or it may be achievement-oriented, depending on the personal characteristics of employees and on the environment. The *Vroom-Yetton-Jago model* suggests that leaders should vary the extent to which they allow employees to participate in decision-making.

The leadership theories outlined above illustrate that management and leadership are related, but they are not the same. In practice, in an era in which the quality of leadership in organisations plays an increasingly important role, the most effective managers are also leaders.

Important terms and concepts

consideration (p.60)
Fiedler's contingency theory (p.64)
Kurt Lewin's leadership styles (p.68)
leadership defined (p.57)
leadership grid (p.60)
leadership versus management (p.69)
least-preferred co-worker (LPC) (p.65)
Michigan continuum (p.59)
Michigan studies (p.59)
Ohio State studies (p.59)
path-goal theory (p.66)
power (p.57)
relationship orientation (p.64)
servant leadership (p.69)
Tannenbaum and Schmidt's leadership continuum (p.62)
task orientation (p.64)
trait theory (p.58)
Vroom-Yetton-Jago contingency theory (p.65)
transformational leadership (p.68)

transactional leadership (p. 69)

Questions for review

1. Discuss the dimensions of leadership with reference to the Ohio State studies, the Michigan studies and the leadership grid.
2. Should the circumstances in which leadership is exercised make a difference to the style of leadership?
3. Write brief notes on:
   a. Fiedler's leadership contingency model
   b. The Vroom-Yetton-Jago contingency theory
   c. The path-goal theory.
4. Analyse the main considerations leaders should take into account when making decisions.
5. Is there a need for leadership in modern-day organisations?

5
ORGANISING AND CONTROLLING

Objectives

This chapter will help you to:

- understand what is meant by organising (in management)
- recognise the link between organising and organisational structure
- explain the nature of control in organisations
- understand the purpose of control within an organisational context
- identify various types of organisational control.

5.1 Organising defined

> Organising is the arrangement of all elements of an organisation to achieve its strategic objectives.

From this definition (Naylor 2004), we can see that organising is concerned with activities such as deciding and choosing the best way to group organisational resources. Organising is the process of designing jobs, grouping jobs into manageable units, and establishing patterns of authority between jobs and units. In relation to the structure of a company, organising involves the assignment of tasks, the grouping of tasks into departments and the allocation of resources to departments. It also involves establishing the flow of authority and communication between positions and levels within an organisation. Organising and planning are closely linked. The organising function typically follows planning and reflects how an organisation tries to accomplish its goals and objectives. Plans state the direction and intentions that managers have for an organisation (see Chapter 3) and organising is the process of co-ordinating individuals and groups in an organisation for the purpose of executing the plans in the most efficient and effective manner in order to achieve organisational goals. The framework used for organising is **organisational structure** (see 5.3 Organisational structure).

5.2 Organising employees

The division of labour in an organisation is the manner in which employees are organised or divided so that different tasks can be performed by different people. **Job specialisation** is an example of the division of labour whereby employees become specialised in specific but limited tasks. The rationale for job specialisation is that it should:

- lead to a more efficient use of labour
- develop employee expertise through repetition of a task
- reduce times for completing tasks as a result of familiarity.

Job specialisation, however, has shown associated disadvantages, such as boredom and dissatisfaction, and its inherent lack of challenge or stimulation can contribute to a rise in absenteeism.

In order to counteract the problems associated with job specialisation, other techniques for the division of labour are often introduced:

- **Job rotation** involves moving employees from one task to another in a systematic way. Employees tend to be more satisfied at first, but satisfaction tends to wane because jobs deemed suitable for rotation tend to be fairly routine.
- **Job enlargement** can be introduced to increase the total number of tasks performed by employees to counteract employee dissatisfaction and lack of motivation which occurs when the same task is repeated. Job enlargement, however, increases training costs and in many instances the tasks remain routine and boring.
- **Job enrichment** increases both the number of tasks an employee performs and the amount of control an employee has in performing tasks. This can be effective as employees who are granted more authority assume a sense of responsibility for the tasks they perform.
- **Work teams** enable employees to decide how tasks will be allocated; they monitor their own progress as a team and have autonomy over the scheduling of tasks.

5.3 Organisational structure

An organisation structure has been defined by Mintzberg (1979) as:

> the sum total of the ways in which it divides its labour into distinct tasks and then achieves co-ordination between them.

The structure of an organisation refers to:

- the size of its hierarchy
- its spans of control
- its division of labour
- its means of co-ordination.

As noted in Chapter 1, **hierarchy** is associated with bureaucratic types of organisations, where there are many layers of management grades between senior managers and junior employees. **Spans of control** refer to the number of employees reporting to a particular supervisor or manager. A narrow span of control means that a small number of employees report to a manager, whereas a wide span means that a large number of employees report to a manager (see Figure 5.1).

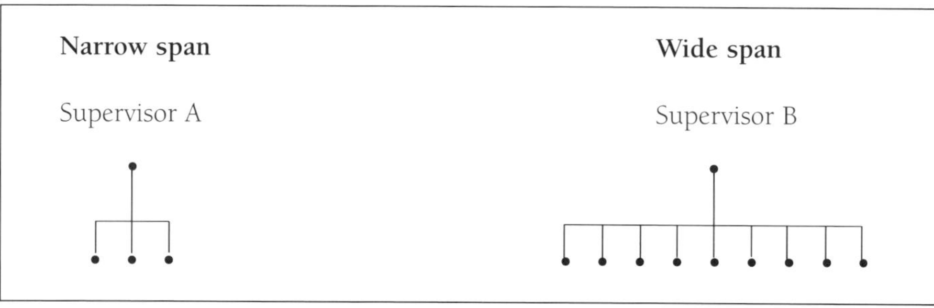

Figure 5.1 Narrow versus wide spans of control

Closely related to the span of control is the **division of labour**. Organisations with wide spans of control and relatively few levels of management grades are called *flat structures*, whereas organisations with narrow spans of control with many managerial levels are called *tall structures* (see Figure 5.2). Mintzberg suggested that the span of control and division of labour depend on the type of task to be performed, whether direct supervision is needed or not, and on the experience of managers and employees.

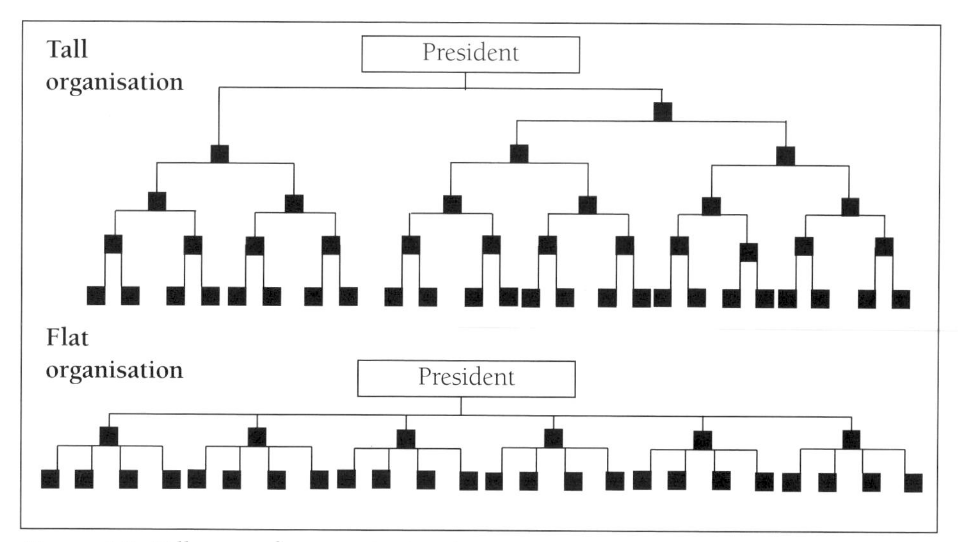

Figure 5.2 Tall versus flat organisational structures

A final element in determining organisational structure is the **co-ordinating activity**. Co-ordinating refers to management activities aimed at achieving an efficient use of resources in order to attain the goals and objectives of an organisation. Many organisations break down the tasks to be performed and co-ordinate these by grouping similar activities together and by forming departments, for example, production, marketing, finance or human resources departments. This is known as **functional departmentalisation** (see Figure 5.3). After departments have been formed, however, the activities of departments must be linked to ensure that all departments are focused on achieving common organisational goals. The co-ordinating activity provides the link between departments because each department depends on the other to perform their respective activities.

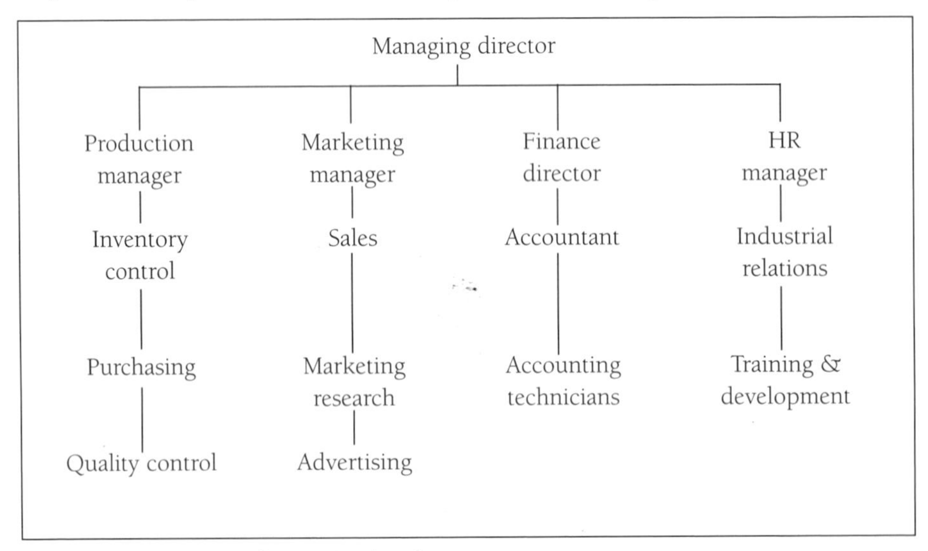

Figure 5.3 Functional organisational structure

Product departmentalisation is another means of co-ordinating activities. This means grouping tasks associated with particular products. Many large organisations that produce a number of products or services divide their activities into business units, with each unit responsible for its own product. Each business unit would have its own set of resources and its own specialist employees. The co-ordinating activity must ensure that each business unit does not focus exclusively on its own product, but that it contributes to the overall goals of the organisation.

A third method of co-ordinating activities is **customer departmentalisation**, which means arranging tasks to respond to and interact with specific customers and their needs. Customer departmentalisation can increase responsiveness to customer needs and can use skilled specialists to deal with individual market segments.

Geographical, or **location**, **departmentalisation** occurs when an organisation structures its activities in various geographical locations. Geographical departmentalisation is suitable for organisations operating in many different countries as it enables organisations to respond to local markets. Geographical departmentalisation, however, requires a large number of managers who can focus on local issues rather than on broader organisational goals.

Strategic business units

Most large organisations are engaged in several businesses, industries and markets. Each business or set of businesses within such an organisation is referred to as a **strategic business unit**. Such units generally are set up as separate companies, with full profit and loss responsibility invested in the top management of the unit. The strategic business units might be based on product lines, geographic markets or other differentiating factors.

Virtual organisations

A virtual organisation has little or no formal structure. A virtual organisation typically has very few permanent employees and a very small administrative headquarters. As the needs of an organisation change, its managers bring in temporary workers, lease facilities and outsource basic support services to meet the demands. The use of computer networks and software designed to facilitate group work within an organisation can speed communications and decision-making. Even more effective is the use of intranets to make company information readily accessible throughout the organisation. The rapid rise of such technology has made virtual organisations and 'boundaryless' organisations possible, where managers, technicians, suppliers, distributors and customers connect digitally rather than physically (see Chapter 10).

5.4 Delegation, decentralisation and centralisation

Another important element of organisational structure is the determination of how authority is to be distributed among positions. **Authority** is power that has been legitimised by the organisation. Specific issues that managers must address when distributing authority include delegation, decentralisation and centralisation.

Delegation is the process by which a manager assigns a portion of his or her total workload to others. The delegation process involves three steps:

- The manager assigns responsibility, or gives the subordinate a job to do.
- Along with the assignment, the individual is also given the authority to do the job.
- The manager establishes the subordinate's accountability, that is, the subordinate accepts an obligation to carry out the task assigned by the manager.

Problems, however, often arise in the delegation process. A manager, for example, may be reluctant to delegate. Some managers may be disorganised so they are unable to plan work in advance, and, as a result, cannot delegate appropriately. Managers may also worry that subordinates will do too well a job and pose a threat to their own positions. On the other hand, some subordinates may be reluctant to accept delegation. They may perceive that there are no rewards for accepting additional responsibility and they may also be concerned that failure will result in a reprimand.

Just as authority can be delegated from one individual to another, organisations also develop patterns of authority across a wide variety of positions and departments. These processes are known as decentralisation and centralisation.

Managers in all organisations have to decide on how much authority to delegate from the top. Griffin (2008) defines **decentralisation** as *the process of systematically delegating power and authority throughout the organisation to middle- and lower-level managers.*

Some advantages of decentralisation:

- Decision-making processes are accelerated as managers do not have to continually refer to top management.
- Motivation is increased as middle and junior managers are given additional responsibilities.
- Top managers can concentrate on the strategic issues of their organisation.

Some disadvantages of decentralisation:

- Managers may place excessive emphasis on their own particular issues rather than working for the interests of the total organisation.
- Customer service can become inconsistent, particularly in service industries.
- An adequate communication system may not be in place to avoid errors.

Overall, most commentators suggest that the advantages of decentralisation outweigh the disadvantages.

Centralisation has been defined by Griffin (2008) as *the process of* *systematically retaining power and authority in the hands of higher-level managers.* In centralised organisations, decisions and responsibility for the whole organisation are retained by top managers.

Some advantages of centralisation:
- it is possible to have a common policy for the whole organisation
- conflict between middle- and lower-level managers can be prevented
- co-ordination and control of the whole organisation is easier to achieve.

Some disadvantages associated with centralisation:
- control and authority may be excessive
- common policies may not be appropriate throughout the whole organisation
- motivation may be inhibited
- initiative may be stifled.

No organisation is ever completely decentralised or completely centralised. There are a number of factors which determine its position. These include:
- *The external environment* — the greater the complexity and uncertainty of the environment, the greater is the tendency to decentralise.
- *History of the organisation* — organisations have a tendency to do what they have done in the past, in terms of decentralisation or centralisation.
- *Nature of the decisions being made* — the costlier and riskier the decision, the more pressure there is to centralise.
- *Ability of lower-level managers* — if lower-level managers have talent and ability, there is likely to be a high level of decentralisation.

5.5 Line and staff

Organising differentiates between *line* and *staff* functions and relationships.

A **line function** contributes *directly* to the achievement of an organisation's primary goals. Line authority is generally thought of as the formal or legitimate authority created by the organisational hierarchy, for example, by production managers exercising control over production staff. An operating manager is an increasingly popular term for someone previously called a line manager. Typical line employees are involved with production and sales.

A **staff function** contributes indirectly to an organisation by supporting line functions and relationships. Staff functions provide expertise and advice, including accounting, purchasing, legal and human resources support for line managers. Staff authority is often exercised through managers having the authority to offer advice/instruction in relation to specialist functions or standards in an organisation. Finance directors and human resources directors, for example, while having responsibility for their respective specialist functions, have the authority to insist that line managers and employees adhere to the organisation's policies in relation to these financial and human resource functions.

Today, however, many organisations have blurred this distinction. New forms of organisation design and a trend toward smaller staff units, for example, have shifted traditional work arrangements. As a result, although human resource activities are still seen as staff functions, line managers often have responsibility devolved to them for carrying out some human resource management functions.

5.6 Control

As discussed in Chapter 1, control is one of the basic functions of management. Control is the regulation of organisational activities in order to achieve organisational objectives and goals. Control keeps an organisation moving in the right direction by measuring actual performance against desired performance. Control can include taking corrective action where needed so that an organisation may reach its targets. The control function is closely linked to the planning and organising functions, as control aims to keep an organisation on an intended course.

Without the control function, organisations have no indication of how well they perform in relation to their goals. At any point in time, the control function will compare where the organisation is in terms of performance (financial, productive or otherwise) to where it is supposed to be. Control provides an organisation with a mechanism for adjusting its course if performance falls outside acceptable boundaries.

The control process

The control process has four fundamental steps (see Figure 5.4):

1. **Establishing standards of performance**. A *control standard* is a target against which subsequent performance will be measured. Standards of performance need to be realistic and clearly stated, for example, in units of production. Control standards should also be consistent with organisational goals.

2. **Measuring performance**. The next step in the control process is to measure performance. The measurement of performance depends on the adequacy, relevance and validity of information generated in an

organisation. Organisations may measure performance on a daily, weekly or monthly basis, for example, through quantifying production units or through sales figures.

3. **Comparing actual results against standards**. The third step in the control process is the comparing of actual results against established standards. Actual results may be higher than the standard, some may be identical and some may be lower. If the actual results are far lower than the standard, organisations may need to review their goals and take corrective action to improve performance.

4. **Determining the need for corrective action**. This is the final step in the control process. If the actual results are far lower than the desired standard, managers may introduce appropriate action to increase performance or they may change the standard. Control, therefore, involves identifying progress and correcting actions to improve overall organisational performance.

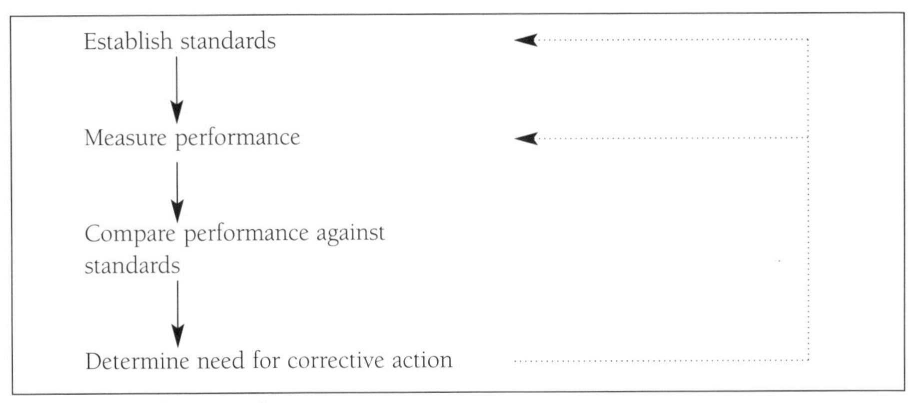

Figure 5.4 The control process

Types of control

There are many methods of control used by organisations. The two main classifications of control are financial or non-financial.

Financial control

Financial control is the control of financial resources as they flow into and out of an organisation. The most commonly used methods of financial control used in organisations are:

- budgetary control

- break-even analysis
- ratio analysis
- financial audits.

Budgetary control. A budget may be defined as *a plan expressed in numerical terms* (Needles *et al.* 1999). The usual time period for a budget is one year, although supplementary monthly or quarter-yearly budgets may also be used. A budget is an action plan for the immediate future of an organisation. Budgetary control takes the targets of desired performance as its standards, then produces information in relation to actual performance and identifies the differences between the desired and actual performance.

Budgets generally use financial data, but they may also be expressed in terms of units of production or sales volume. Budgets enable performance to be measured across departments, through various hierarchical levels in an organisation, and from one period to another. Budgets may be further subdivided into *financial*, *operating* and *non-monetary*, as illustrated in Table 5.1.

Financial budget	***What each budget illustrates***
Cash budget	Cash income and cash expenditure.
Capital expenditure budget	Costs of major assets, for example, new building, machinery.
Balance sheet budget	Forecast of an organisation's assets and liabilities.
Operating budget	
Sales budget	An organisation's income from its activities.
Expense budget	Projected expenses for an organisation.
Profit budget	Projected differences between sales and expenses.
Non-monetary budget	
Labour budget	Number of employee hours available for use.
Production budget	Number of units to be produced.
Space budget	Floor space available for various departments or functions.

Table 5.1 Types of budget

Generally, the main aims of budgetary control are to:

- establish short-term business plans
- assess progress in achieving short-term plans
- ensure co-ordination between various departments in an organisation.

Information provided from various sources, for example, sales, production, capital expenditure and cash, are gathered to form a master budget, which is a statement of budgeted profit and loss together with a projected balance sheet.

Break-even analysis. The second financial control is called break-even analysis which involves the use of fixed and variable costs to analyse the break-even point at which it becomes profitable to produce a good or service.

Fixed costs (also known as *overheads*) are costs that do not vary with production or sales levels. For example, regardless of production output, an organisation must pay bills for rent, power, interest and salaries. Fixed costs occur regardless of variable costs.

Variable costs vary directly with levels of production. They are called variable because their total varies with the number of units produced.

Total costs are the sum of the fixed and variable costs for any given level of production.

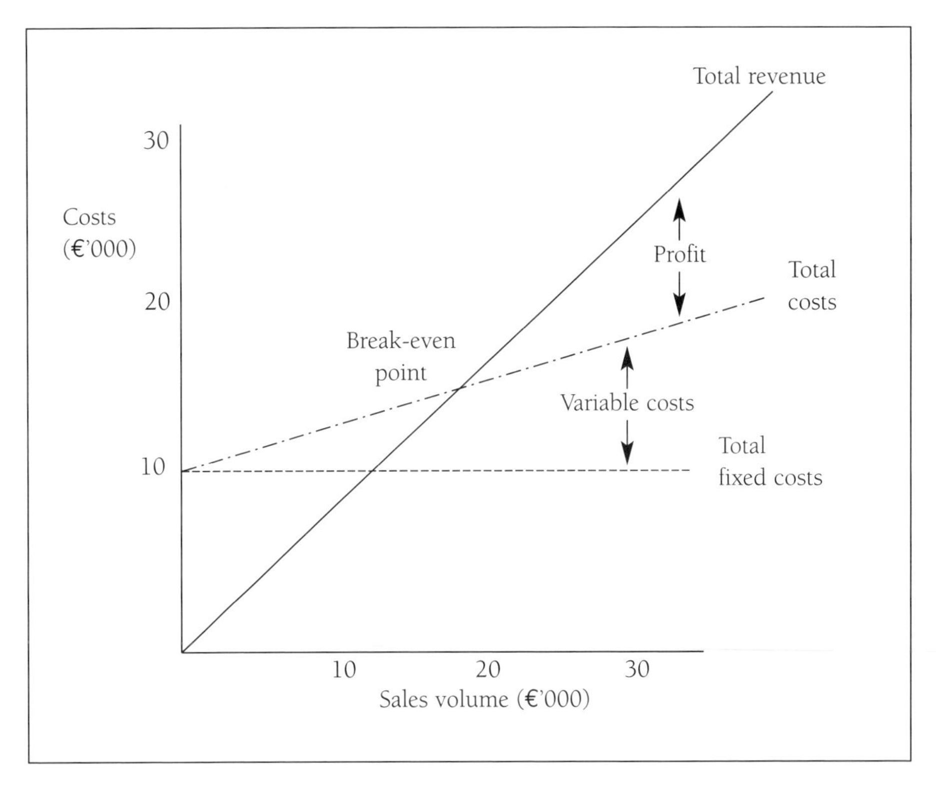

Figure 5.5 Break-even chart

When managers analyse the level of both fixed and variable costs, they can identify the volume needed to break even, and this information can be made available on a break-even chart (see, for example, Figure 5.5). A break-even chart illustrates how costs and profits vary with the volume of production. The break-even point on the chart is where the total costs line crosses the sales revenue, and that is the point where neither a profit or loss is made.

In the example in Figure 5.5, total costs (*fixed costs plus variable costs*) range from €10,000 to €20,000. Total revenue ranges from zero to €30,000. The break-even point is achieved when a sales volume of about €16,000 is reached. Sales in excess of this figure produce a profit.

Overall, break-even charts indicate the effects on profits of marginal changes in sales volume or in costs. The charts provide a graphic illustration of how much should be produced before profits can be made. The straight lines on the charts, however, may be over-simplistic, therefore, break-even analysis should be used in tandem with other control mechanisms for greater accuracy.

Ratio analysis. Another aspect of financial control is the analysis of performance data. A *ratio* provides a useful tool for this type of analysis. Financial ratios are relationships that exist between accounting figures, and are usually expressed in percentage terms.

Ratio analysis allows an organisation to monitor its performance over time and to compare it with competitor performance. Some examples of financial ratios are:

- Net profit margin $= \dfrac{\text{Net profit}}{\text{Sales}} \times 100$
- Current ratio (liquidity) $= \dfrac{\text{Current assets}}{\text{Current liabilities}}$

Ratios can provide useful information regarding the progress or efficiency of an organisation, particularly when comparisons are made with competitors. As with break-even analysis, ratios should be used in conjunction with other methods of performance analysis.

Financial audits are independent appraisals of an organisation's accounting, financial and operational systems. The two major types of financial audit are the external audit and the internal audit.

External audits are financial appraisals conducted by experts who are not employees of the organisation. External audits are typically concerned with ensuring that the organisation's accounting procedures and financial statements are compiled in an objective and verifiable fashion. The organisation contracts certified public accountants for this service.

Internal audits are handled by employees of the organisation. Its objective is the same as that of an external audit — to verify the accuracy of financial and accounting procedures used by the organisation. Internal audits also examine the efficiency and appropriateness of financial and accounting procedures.

Non-financial controls

In addition to financial control, organisations may also utilise a number of non-financial control mechanisms.

Quality control. The role of quality control is to ensure that appropriate standards of quality are set and that deviations from particular standards are rejected. Quality control is, therefore, a system for setting quality standards, measuring performance against those standards and taking appropriate action to deal with any deviations from those standards. Benefits of quality control include:

- limiting the accumulation of errors
- reduction in costs of reworking
- reduction in customer complaints
- improved reputation for an organisation's products.

Quality assurance. This refers to the systematic monitoring and evaluation of the various aspects of a project, service or facility to ensure that standards of quality are being met. Two key principles characterise quality assurance: 'fit for purpose' (the product should be suitable for the intended purpose) and 'right first time' (mistakes should be eliminated). Quality assurance includes regulation of the quality of raw materials, assemblies, products and components; services related to production; and management, production and inspection processes.

Inventory control. Inventory control involves controlling stock levels to ensure that an organisation has an adequate amount of stock to produce goods, while at the same time not having too much money tied up in stock which may not be required immediately. Developments in information technology for inventory tracking have helped to reduce excessive stock holding, while also automatically monitoring stock depletions for restocking purposes.

Production control. This is closely related to inventory and quality control. The aim of production control is to enable products to be provided on time, and that they are made available and affordable. The product control concept implies, first, that customers will favour products that offer the most quality, performance and features and, second, that organisations should devote energy to making continuous product improvements. Developments in information technology can enhance production control by monitoring errors per hour and measuring machine speeds and employee productivity.

Total Quality Management (TQM). Total Quality Management (TQM) is a concept that links policy and operational practice. Of the three elements of TQM:

- *Total* suggests full commitment of everyone in the organisation and coverage of every aspect of all processes.
- *Quality* means continuously meeting customers' requirements.
- *Management* implies an active process led from the top.

The basis of TQM is to reduce the errors produced during the manufacturing or service process, increase customer satisfaction, streamline supply chain management, aim for modernisation of equipment and ensure workers have the highest level of training. One of the main aims of TQM is to limit errors to one per one million units produced.

5.7 Managing control in organisations

For control systems to be effective in organisations, they need to be:

- *Linked with planning* — for example, when goals are set, control mechanisms should be an integral part of planning to achieve goals.
- *Flexible* — for example, inventory control must be capable of accommodating changes in quantities of raw materials.
- *Objective* — for example, the control system should provide information that is as objective as possible for managers.
- *Timely* — for example, when information is needed for control purposes, it must be available as often as is necessary.

Managers should realise that employees may resist control, particularly if they believe they are over-controlled. The extent of resistance depends on the balance of the control system, its design and the manner and the circumstances in which control is implemented. Mullins (2007) proposes that resistance to control will be greater when the control system:

- measures performance in a new area

- replaces a system that people have an interest in retaining
- uses standards that are set without participation
- does not feed results to those whose performance is measured
- feeds results to higher levels in an organisation
- provides results to be used by the reward system
- affects people who are satisfied with the way things are and who regard themselves as committed to an organisation's aims
- affects people who have low self-esteem.

Managers, however, can help overcome resistance to control by encouraging employee participation in planning and in implementing the control system. The control function is often controversial because the benefits of control systems are not always obvious to employees. Managers should ensure that employees recognise that control mechanisms are effective, properly integrated with organisational planning, flexible, accurate, timely and objective.

5.8 Key points

Organisational structure refers to the division of employees and of tasks. Employees may be organised in various ways, for example, according to:
- job specialisation
- job rotation
- job enlargement
- job enrichment
- work teams.

Organisational tasks may be organised through:
- functional departmentalisation
- product departmentalisation
- customer departmentalisation
- geographical departmentalisation.

Organisations develop patterns of distributing authority across a wide variety of departments and positions. This distribution of authority can be thought of as a continuum with *decentralisation* at one end and *centralisation* at the other end. No organisation is completely decentralised or centralised.

The managerial function of *control* is closely linked to the functions of planning and organising. Financial and non-financial control is concerned with regulating organisational activities to minimise errors and to achieve organisational goals more efficiently and effectively.

The *control process* consists of four steps:

- establishing standards of performance
- measuring performance
- comparing actual results against standards
- determining the need for corrective action.

Employees may resist control if they perceive that they are being over-controlled. Managers can overcome this resistance by improving the effectiveness of controls and by increasing employee participation in developing control processes.

Important terms and concepts

authority (p.79)
break-even analysis (p.85)
budgetary control (p.84)
centralisation (p.80)
control (p.82)
control process (p.82)
customer departmentalisation (p.78)
decentralisation (p.80)
delegation (p.80)
financial audit (p.86)
financial control (p.83)
flat structure (p.77)
functional departmentalisation (p.78)
geographical departmentalisation (p.79)
inventory control (p.87)
job enlargement (p.76)
job enrichment (p.76)
job rotation (p.76)
job specialisation (p.76)
line and staff (p.81)
organisational structure (p.76)
organising defined (p.75)
product departmentalisation (p.78)
production control (p.88)
quality assurance (p.87)
quality control (p.87)
ratio analysis (p.86)
strategic business units (p.79)

tall structure (p.77)
virtual organisations (p.79)
work teams (p.76)

Questions for review

1. Write brief notes on:
   a. Job specialisation
   b. Job rotation
   c. Job enlargement
   d. Job enrichment.

2. Explain the link between the organising function and the organisational structure.

3. Describe the management function of control.

4. Write brief notes on:
   a. Delegation, centralisation and decentralisation
   b. Span of control
   c. Resistance to control in organisations.

5. Discuss two commonly used methods of control in organisations.

6 COMMUNICATION

Objectives

This chapter will help you to:

- define communication and recognise its importance for every manager
- recognise the characteristics of useful information
- understand the communication process
- identify the barriers to effective communication
- explain how to overcome barriers to effective communication.

6.1 Communication defined

Organisational communication can be defined as (ACAS 1982):

> the provision and passing of information and instructions which enable a company or any employing organisation to function efficiently and employees to be properly informed about developments. It covers information of all kinds which can be provided; the channels along which it passes; and the means of passing it.

Griffin (2008) defined communication as *the process of transmitting information from one person to another*. From these two definitions, it is evident that communication is a process of creating, transmitting and interpreting information between two or more people.

Effective communication, then, is the process of sending a message so that the message received is as close in meaning as possible to the message intended. Effective communication is based on the ideas of meaning and consistency of meaning. *Meaning* is the idea which the individual who initiates the communication exchange wishes to convey. With effective communication the meaning is transmitted in such a way that the receiving person properly understands the exchange.

6.2 The purposes of communication in organisations

Communication among individuals and groups is vital in all organisations. The primary purpose of communication is **to achieve co-ordinated action.**

Without communication, an organisation would be merely a collection of individual employees doing separate tasks. Organisational action would lack co-ordination and be oriented toward individual rather than organisational goals.

A second purpose of communication is **information sharing**, for example, information relating to organisational goals, which give employees a sense of purpose and direction. Another information-sharing function of communication is to give specific task directions to individuals. Information on organisational goals gives employees a sense of how their activities fit into the overall picture; task communication tells them what their job duties are and are not. Employees should also receive information on the results of their efforts, as in performance appraisals.

Communication is also essential to the **decision-making process**, as discussed in Chapter 3. Information, and thus information sharing, is needed to define problems, generate and evaluate alternatives, implement decisions, and control and evaluate results.

Communication also relates directly to the basic management functions of **planning**, **organising**, **leading** and **controlling**. Delegation, co-ordination, and organisational change and development also entail communication. Developing reward systems and interacting with subordinates as part of the leading function would be impossible without some form of communication. Communication is also essential to establishing standards, monitoring performance and taking corrective actions as part of control.

Finally, communication **expresses feelings and emotions**. Organisational communication is far from a collection of facts and figures. People in organisations, like people anywhere else, need to communicate emotions such as happiness, anger, displeasure, confidence and fear. Clearly, then, communication is a pervasive part of virtually all managerial activities.

6.3 Characteristics of useful information

According to Mintzberg (1973), managers spend over half of their daily work schedule communicating; a typical day would include attending scheduled and unscheduled meetings, making and receiving telephone calls, and writing, reading and answering correspondence. As communication is a large part of a manager's daily work life, it is important that the information that is being communicated is useful.

Useful communication generally has four attributes. It should be:

- *Accurate* — the information being transmitted must provide a manager with real and valid facts; for example, a balance sheet should illustrate the accurate financial position of an organisation.

- *Timely* — the information has to be available in time for managers to choose an appropriate course of action; for example, if a manager is sitting on an interview board, he or she needs to have copies of the relevant details of candidates selected for interview in advance.
- *Complete* — the information should enable a manager to understand the full context of a situation. Where information is incomplete, a manager may hold an inaccurate account of an organisation or context. A financial controller, for example, will require information on the financial situation of all departments in order to assess the overall financial state of a particular organisation.
- *Relevant* — if the information is to be useful, it must be relevant to the circumstances of the particular managers involved; for example, production managers require details on levels of production achieved, whereas marketing managers require details on advertising rates and sales.

6.4 Types of communication in organisations

Organisational communication consists of **informal communication**, which includes 'grapevine' rumours, gossip and general conversation, and **formal communication**, whether written, oral or graphic.

To decide which method of communication is most effective for information, managers generally need to ask themselves:

- *What* needs to be communicated?
- *When* should something be communicated?
- *How* should something be communicated?
- *Where* should communication be held?
- *Who* should be communicated with?

Oral communication consists of face-to-face conversation, telephone calls, formal presentations, departmental meetings, teleconferencing and group discussions. Oral communication is the most prevalent form of organisational communication. Oral communication is particularly powerful because it includes not only speakers' words but also their changes in tone, pitch, speed and volume. As listeners, people use all of these cues to understand oral messages.

The primary advantage of oral communication is that it promotes prompt feedback and interchange in the form of verbal questions or agreement, facial expressions and gestures. Oral communication is typically easy (as all the sender needs to do is talk), and it can be done with little preparation. Oral communication, however, has drawbacks. It may suffer from problems of inaccuracy if the speaker chooses the wrong words to convey meaning or leaves out pertinent details, if noise disrupts the process, or if the receiver forgets part or the entire message. A two-way discussion seldom allows time for a thoughtful, considered response, or for introducing many new facts, and there is no permanent record of what has been said. It allows for immediate feedback and re-explanation but it may suffer from misinterpretation and inaccuracy if the speaker chooses inappropriate words to convey information. The popular voicemail has all the characteristics of traditional verbal communication except there is no feedback. The sender just leaves the message on the machine with no feedback or confirmation that the message was, or will be, received. With no confirmation, the sender does not know for sure that the message will be received as the sender intended it.

Written communication consists of memos, letters, notes, e-mails, company newspapers, noticeboards, company reports, internal and external post, the Internet, and corporate intranets. Following up with a written summary can solve many of the problems of oral communication. Written communication can be accurate and provides a record of the information exchanged. The information can be drafted and revised by the sender before it is transmitted, and the receiver can take time to reread it if necessary. Written communication, however, is slower with regard to feedback and the exchange of ideas.

The biggest single drawback of written communication is that it inhibits immediate feedback and interchange. If there is a misunderstanding, it will take longer to recognise and rectify it.

Non-verbal communication consists of any communication that does not use words. It relies on facial expression, gestures, body movements and physical contact, and is a powerful form of communication. A study by Eisenhardt *et al.* (1997) found that words accounted for only 7 per cent of the content of the message, whereas 55 per cent of the content was transmitted by facial expression and body language and another 38 per cent was transmitted by tone.

Electronic communication has taken on much greater importance in organisations in recent years. Both formal information systems and personal information technology have reshaped how people communicate with one another. E-mail systems, the Internet, corporate intranets and teleconferences all help to clarify and speed communication in organisations.

Choosing a form of communication depends on a particular situation. For example, oral communication is suited to personal, short communications and non-routine situations; written communication is suited to impersonal, longer communications and routine situations. Managers often combine oral and written communication.

Meetings

Conducting a meeting is an important managerial skill. Meetings often form a vital link between staff and the organisation. This is particularly true for those who work off site, such as sales and service crews, out-reach workers and home workers. Common complaints are that meetings are boring, wastes of time, lack direction, never achieve anything, go over old issues and offer an opportunity for a manager to give a lecture. A number of elements contribute to ensuring that meetings are conducted more efficiently and effectively. These include:

- *Have a clear objective* — start the meeting on time and do not reward latecomers by delaying the meeting. Ensure that the same results, such as giving instructions, could not be achieved elsewhere.
- *Invite only those who are needed* — others become frustrated and may be disruptive. There are a number of possible inclusions: the decision-makers, the implementers, those affected and those with information.
- *Choose an appropriate venue* — make sure it is comfortable, quiet, uninterrupted and has appropriate equipment.
- *Issue an agenda in advance* — the agenda is the plan of the meeting and it should be sent out in time to allow everyone time to prepare for the meeting. Keep the number of items realistic as there is no point in trying to cover too much.
- *Choose an effective chairperson* — the role of the chairperson is to control the meeting and to encourage participation. The chairperson follows the agenda to ensure that everything is addressed. He or she will clarify points, summarise positions and seek consensus.
- *Conclude, summarise, and evaluate* — set aside some time to discuss how effective the meeting was and how it might be improved.

6.5 The flow of communication in organisations

Communication is frequently classified by its route in organisations — downward, upward and horizontal being the most common classifications.

Downward communication (top-down) occurs when information comes down the hierarchy from managers to employees. Examples of downward communication are:

- company newspapers
- employee reports
- general information that higher-level managers think will be of value to lower-level managers and employees.

Upward communication occurs when messages are sent from employees to managers. Examples of upward communication are:
- suggestion schemes
- questionnaires
- surveys.

Upward communication is usually passed through an immediate supervisor, to a lower-level manager and then to higher-level managers.

Horizontal communication occurs between individuals and teams or between departments and work groups and involves colleagues and peers at the same level in an organisation. Organisations with flatter structures tend to make greater use of horizontal communication between employees who work on similar tasks or specialised situations.

Horizontal communication serves a number of purposes:
- It facilitates co-ordination among interdependent departments.
- It can be used for joint problem-solving.
- It plays a major role in work teams whose members are drawn from several departments.

6.6 Steps in developing effective communication

Managers need to understand the steps involved in the communication process in order to ensure that their communication process is effective. There are nine elements in the communication process, with the *sender* and *receiver* being the key elements (see Figure 6.1):

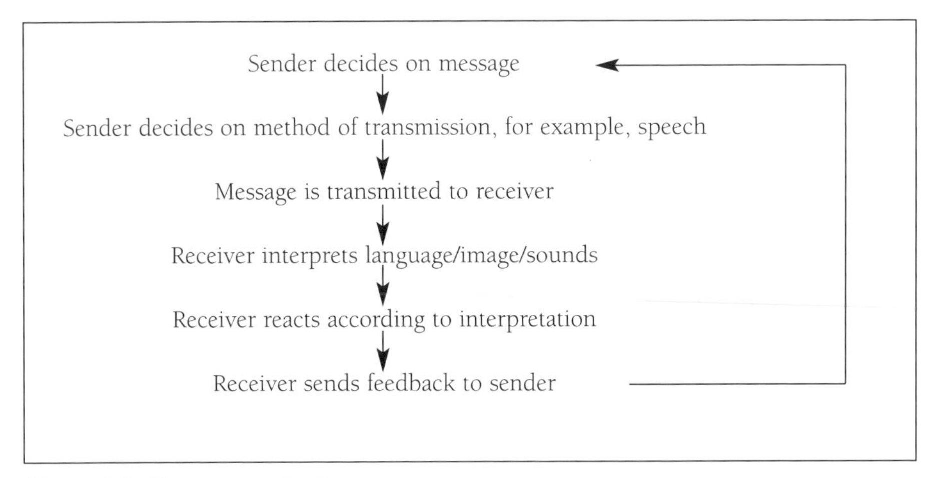

Figure 6.1 The communication process

- *Sender* — a person (the sender) transmitting a message to someone, for example, a manager notifying employees regarding a training course.
- *Encoding* — the process of conveying the intended message through, for example, words, illustrations and body language.
- *Message* — the actual information which, for example, might contain the time, date, location and content of a seminar and details of the presenters.
- *Media* — the communication channels through which a message moves from sender to receiver, for example, e-mails, letters, telephone calls, memos.
- *Decoding* — interpretations of a message by those receiving the message; the content and the perceived relevance of the communication influence the decoding.
- *Receiver* — the person receiving the message.
- *Response* — the reactions of the receiver, for example, employees may react positively, neutrally, sceptically or negatively.
- *Feedback* — the receiver's response communicated to the sender.
- *Noise* — unplanned distortion during the process which may disrupt communication, for example, passing on mistaken recollections of an original message

6.7 Barriers to effective communication

Communication skills are important for all managers. There are, however, numerous factors that may hinder communication or act as barriers to effective communication, the most common ones being:

- *Predispositions and individual bias* — receivers of communications may already have their minds firmly set in a certain way or may have a bias influenced by cultural background or personal values.
- *Reluctance to communicate* — employees may be reluctant to communicate with their manager because of fear, or because they believe their manager does not value their opinions.
- *Information overload* — employees may be receiving more information than they can effectively handle.
- *Status differences* — higher-level managers, for example, may not be interested in hearing what new employees have to say.
- *Poor listening skills* — individuals may not have developed their listening skills, resulting in, for example, delegates at a meeting not paying attention and failing to recall what has been said.
- *Noise* — any unintended interference with effective communication; noise may include sounds, or other distractions not associated with sound, that

are not relevant to a communication, such as visual distractions, talk from other employees, emotional upsets or physical discomfort.
- *Verbal difficulties* — for example, the use of jargon or technical words which the receiver may not understand.

Overcoming the barriers to successful communication

The following methods help to overcome barriers to communication:
- *Predispositions and individual bias* — individuals should be encouraged to approach communication with an open mind and be willing to change their views; people are often unaware of their own biases until they are brought to their attention.
- *Reluctance to communicate* — a 'blame-free' organisational culture will encourage employees to communicate freely and will demonstrate that employees' opinions are valued.
- *Information overload* — the amount of communication transmitted to employees should be limited and communication should always be relevant and appropriate to employee needs.
- *Status differences* — upward communication should be valued and employees actively encouraged to communicate across all levels of an organisation.
- *Poor listening skills* — proactive listening skills should be learned; essentially, this means not interrupting the speaker, concentrating on the speaker's words and their meaning, listening with patience, and showing interest.
- *Noise* — improvements in the working environment and attempts to eliminate distractions may be required.
- *Verbal difficulties* — the language used should be clear and easy to understand and jargon and over-technical language should be avoided.

6.8 Key points

Communication is the process of transmitting information from one person to another. *Effective communication* is the process of a sender transmitting a message to a receiver in such a way that the message is received as close in meaning as possible to the message intended.

Various forms of communication are used in organisations. These include oral, written and non-verbal communication. Organisational communication may be formal or informal. *Vertical communication* between managers and employees may be both upward and downward. *Horizontal communication* involves colleagues at the same level communicating.

If the information to be communicated is to be useful, it must be accurate, timely, complete and relevant. In order for communication to be effective it is important that the sender clearly encodes the message and transmits it accurately to one or more receivers, who receive the message and decode it into meaning.

There are a number of *barriers* that hinder the communication process. Managers need to recognise these barriers and understand how to overcome them. Generally barriers can be identified at both the individual and organisational level. Similarly, individual and organisational solutions may be used to overcome these barriers.

Important terms and concepts

barriers to communication (p.98)
characteristics of useful information (p.93)
co-ordinated action (p.92)
communication defined (p.92)
decoding (p.98)
decision-making process (p.93)
downward communication (p.96)
effective communication (p.92)
electronic communication (p.95)
encoding (p.98)
feedback (p.98)
horizontal communication (p.97)
media (p.98)
meetings (p.96)
message (p.98)
noise (p.98)
non-verbal communication (p.95)
oral communication (p.94)
overcoming barriers to successful communication (p.99)
planning, organising, leading and controlling (p.93)
purposes of communication (p.92)
receiver (p.98)
response (p.98)
sender (p.98)
upward communication (p.97)
written communication (p.95)

Questions for review

1. Evaluate the importance of effective communication in a rapidly expanding organisation which is undergoing growth and technological changes in its product range.

2. a. Describe barriers to effective communication in an organisation.
   b. Suggest how these barriers might be overcome.

3. Explain how a manager can combine oral, written and non-verbal communication into an effective communication system.

4. Discuss the advantages of effective communications in business.

5. What are the components of the communication process?

7 MOTIVATION

Objectives

This chapter will help you to:

- explain what motivation is
- describe the major *content* perspectives on motivation
- describe the major *process* perspectives on motivation
- highlight the motivating characteristics common to a number of motivational theories.

7.1 Motivation defined

The word motivation is coined from the Latin word *movere*, which means to move. Motivation theory is concerned with the processes that describe why and how human behaviour is activated and directed. It is regarded as one of the most important areas of study in the field of organisational behaviour.

Motivation has been defined by Steers and Porter (1991) as:

> the set of forces that cause people to behave in certain ways.

Motivation theorists aim to discover the motive, or drive, that triggers and sustains particular behaviours of individuals. Motivation refers to both the *internal* and *external* forces that direct people's behaviour.

The study of motivation is important for managers as motivated staff work well. Work motivation is a psychological concept that is primarily concerned with increasing the direction of employees' work-related behaviours to positively influence performance output. There are many theories of motivation, but there is no simple answer to the question 'How do you motivate employees?'

7.2 Historical perspectives on motivation

The **traditional approach** to motivation is best represented by the work of Frederick W. Taylor. As noted in Chapter 1, Taylor advocated an incentive pay system. He believed that managers knew more about the jobs being performed than did workers, and he assumed that money was the primary motivator for everyone. Other assumptions of the traditional approach were that work is unpleasant for most people and that the money they earn is more important than the nature of the job they are performing. Hence, people could be expected to perform any kind of job if they are paid enough. Although the role of money as a motivating factor cannot be dismissed today, the traditional approach took too narrow a view of the role of monetary compensation and also failed to consider other motivational factors.

The **human relations approach** emphasised the role of social processes in the workplace (Chapter 1). Human relations theorists emphasised that employees want to feel useful and important, that employees have strong social needs (e.g. friends at work), and that these needs are more important than money in motivating employees. Proponents of the human relations approach advised managers to motivate employees by allowing them self-direction and self-control in carrying out activities.

The human resource approach

The human resource approach to motivation assumes that employees are motivated by their contribution and participation and that these are valuable to both individuals and organisations. **Participation** is the process of giving employees a voice in making decisions about their work. The human resource approach assumes that employees want to contribute and are able to make genuine contributions. The task of managers, therefore, is to encourage participation and to create a work environment which makes full use of the human resources available. This approach guides most contemporary thinking about employee motivation.

Closely linked with participation is empowerment. **Empowerment** is the process of enabling workers to set their own work goals, make decisions, and solve problems within their sphere of responsibility and authority. Empowerment promotes participation in many areas including the work itself, work context and work environment.

7.3 Motivational theories

Motivation theories analyse employee performance and how work, and its rewards, satisfy individual employee needs. Employees have basic needs or expectations which, if not satisfied, stimulate behaviour directed towards satisfying those needs. One basic model of motivation suggests the presence of a stimulus (a physical drive or need), followed by a behaviour of some kind which leads to a satisfactory or unsatisfactory response or outcome (Figure 7.1).

Motivational theories are generally divided into content and process theories. **Content theories** concentrate on *what* motivates people, for example, the factors that motivate people. **Process theories** concentrate on *why* people choose to behave in certain ways and how motivation is aroused and maintained.

Figure 7.1 Basic model of motivation

Content theories of motivation

Maslow's hierarchy of needs

During the 1940s, Abraham Maslow, an American organisational psychologist, was one of the first to classify human needs or motives. Maslow suggested that human needs may be classified into motivating factors that influence behaviour. He proposed that these needs are based on a hierarchical model, with basic needs at the bottom and higher needs at the top (see Figure 7.2).

According to Maslow's hierarchy, most people are motivated by the desire to satisfy a group of five specific needs. Starting from the bottom of the hierarchy, these needs are:

- *Physiological needs* — for example, food, sleep and air, which represent basic requirements of survival; in an organisational setting, examples of these needs include:
  - salary
  - comfortable temperatures
  - adequate lighting
  - an environment generally conducive to work.
- *Safety and security needs* — for example, a stable and secure physical and emotional environment; in an organisational setting, examples of these needs are:
  - job continuity
  - a pension plan
  - a grievance system.
- *Belongingness needs* — for example, the need for love, friendship and acceptance; in an organisational setting, examples of these needs are:
  - friends at work
  - teamwork
  - social interaction at work.
- *Esteem needs* — for example, the need for a positive self-image, self-esteem, status, and the need for recognition and respect from others; in

an organisational setting, examples of these needs are:
  - a sense of accomplishment
  - a job title.
- *Self-actualisation needs* — for example, the need for self-fulfilment, achievement and continued individual development; in an organisational setting, these needs can be met by:
  - a challenging job
  - participation in making decisions about one's work
  - opportunities for further learning
  - activities that contribute to a sense of fulfilment.

Maslow believed that people tend to satisfy their needs systematically, beginning with the basic physiological needs and then moving up the hierarchy. Maslow further suggested that as long as physiological needs remain unsatisfied, an individual is motivated only to fulfil them. When physiological needs have been satisfied, an individual then moves 'up' the hierarchy and is concerned with safety and security needs. The individual continues to move 'up' until self-actualisation level needs are reached.

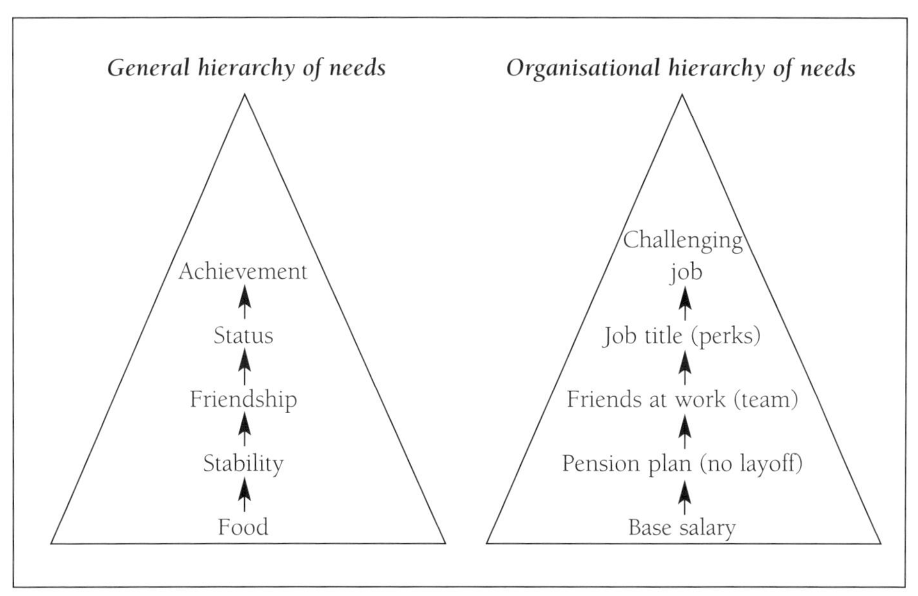

Figure 7.2 Maslow's hierarchy of needs

A frequent criticism of Maslow's theory is that, at any given time, different people are likely to be striving to fulfil different need levels of the hierarchy. The model assumes that one motive or drive should predominate at any moment in time, whereas individuals may actually be working simultaneously for pay (security), social interaction (belongingness) and status (self-esteem). Some individuals may also choose to satisfy their needs outside their workplace, for example, through sport or other leisure activities. Maslow's theory, however, has illustrated that people have a variety of needs, the satisfaction of which may be pursued at work, and managers need to understand these needs in order to motivate employees.

Alderfer's ERG model

A variation of Maslow's model was proposed by Alderfer in 1969, arguing that individual needs were best explained on a continuum, rather than in a hierarchy. Alderfer believed that there are only three major sets of needs:

- *Existence needs* (E) — for example, the basic requirements of life, that is, a combination of Maslow's physiological and safety needs.
- *Relatedness needs* (R) — for example, social and interpersonal needs, reflecting Maslow's social or belongingness needs level.
- *Growth needs* (G) — for example, personal development needs; this is a combination of Maslow's self-esteem and self-actualisation needs.

Alderfer's research findings, based on 110 questionnaires distributed to bank officials of various levels, suggested that the less a higher-order need was satisfied the more likely it was that an individual would revert to satisfying the next level of need below, even though it had previously been satisfied. Alderfer concluded, therefore, that needs are not determined hierarchically.

McClelland's achievement motivation

Research conducted by David McClelland (1961) of Harvard University stresses the importance of individual differences in motivation. McClelland and his team conducted research with over five hundred managers from twenty-five different organisations in the United States to determine what motivates a good manager. Their research findings suggest that managers possess three basic motivational needs:

- need for achievement (n-Ach)
- need for power (n-Pow)
- need for affiliation (n-Aff).

McClelland believed that managers who have a high need for achievement (n-Ach) are influenced by childhood experiences that gave them independence at an early age and by cultural backgrounds that expected competence from them. He concluded that, if the need for achievement is strongly influenced by environmental factors, employees can be motivated to achieve through training programmes. McClelland also stated that managers with a high need for achievement will be attracted to entrepreneurial rather than bureaucratic organisations.

McClelland found that managers who did not score high on the need for achievement may score high on the need for affiliation (n-Aff), meaning that these managers will be concerned with having approval from both their employees and superiors and will be sensitive to the needs of others. He also suggested that managers who are concerned with the needs of others are still interested in getting the job done, which in turn should lead to greater organisational effectiveness.

McClelland's research also illustrated that good interpersonal skills are important for managers, particularly when combined with a need to influence people for the overall good of an organisation. Managers who forcefully express their opinions and who like being in control of events have a greater need for power (n-Pow) than the need to achieve or to be liked. The concept of power in organisations is closely linked to leadership; for example, McClelland suggested that higher-level managers in organisations tended to be associated with a low level of affiliation and a moderate-to-high need for power.

Overall, McClelland's research is important as it recognises that people do not share similar needs to the same extent. His research findings also proposed that some important needs are not inherited but learned. In comparison with other content theories of motivation, McClelland's work looks more towards the development of senior managers.

Herzberg's two-factor theory

Frederick Herzberg (1959) developed his two-factor theory of motivation by concentrating on satisfaction at work. Herzberg and his team interviewed two hundred accountants and engineers and asked them to recall when they had experienced satisfactory and unsatisfactory feelings about their jobs.

The research concluded that two different factors affect motivation at work. The factors influencing satisfaction are called *motivation factors* and are specifically related to the content of the work involved. The factors which remove dissatisfaction are called *hygiene factors* and are related to the adequacy of work conditions. The research suggested that, while hygiene factors help to remove dissatisfaction, they do not necessarily provide satisfaction as the absence of dissatisfaction does not equate to satisfaction. Motivation factors, on the other hand, push individuals to achieve greater performance (see Table 7.1).

Herzberg suggested that hygiene factors and dissatisfiers (the lack of hygiene factors) were related more to the environment than to work content. The major difference between hygiene and motivators is that adequate hygiene factors can prevent dissatisfaction, whereas motivators can bring positive satisfaction. Employees generally assume that hygiene factors should be in place and may take them for granted, but if they are not, employees tend to be dissatisfied.

Motivation factors	*Hygiene factors*
• Achievement • Recognition • Work itself • Responsibility	• Working conditions • Company policies and administration • Interpersonal relationships • Pay and security

Table 7.1 Motivation and hygiene factors

A criticism of Herzberg's theory is that his sample of accountants and engineers was not representative of the general population, and his theories need further research to prove their validity generally. The theory, however, has led to designing jobs containing a greater number of motivators.

McGregor's Theory X and Theory Y

McGregor's Theory X and Theory Y (1960) are classifications of two sets of assumptions about behaviour. McGregor believed that managers classified employee behaviour as either Theory X or Theory Y, as illustrated in Table 7.2.

Theory X	*Theory Y*
Employees are lazy and dislike work.	Employees like work.
Employees need to be controlled and coerced.	Employees do not have to be controlled or coerced.
Employees dislike responsibility.	Employees accept and seek responsibility.
Employees want only security and material rewards.	Employees want intrinsic rewards and are creative and imaginative.

Table 7.2 Theory X, Theory Y

McGregor argued that Theory X represented the views of scientific management theorists and Theory Y represented the human relations approach. He suggested that, under the right conditions, Theory Y managers could motivate staff to exercise self-direction and control and to apply their intellect to problems as they arise. Theory X and Theory Y identify two extreme forms of management style. A mixture of the two styles, however, is likely to produce a more effective managerial approach.

Process theories of motivation

Equity theory

Equity theory attempts to explain satisfaction in terms of perceptions of fair/unfair distributions of resources within interpersonal relationships. Equity theory was first developed in 1963 by John Stacey Adams, a workplace and behavioural psychologist.

When employees are motivated to behave in certain ways, they assess the fairness or equity of their behaviour. Equity theory matches the notion of 'an honest day's work for an honest day's pay'. Equity is an employee's belief that the treatment or reward he or she receives is equitable to the treatment that other employees receive. Employees assess their inputs, such as education, experience and effort in relation to the outcomes they receive, including pay, promotional prospects, benefits and recognition. Equity theory proposes that employees view their incomes and outcomes as a ratio and then compare their ratio to that of another employee or other employees with similar circumstances:

$$\frac{\text{Outcomes (self)}}{\text{Inputs (self)}} = (?) \frac{\text{Outcomes (other)}}{\text{Inputs (other)}}$$

Inputs are viewed as an individual's contribution to the exchange and are viewed as entitling him/her to rewards or costs. The inputs that an employee contributes to a relationship can be either assets — entitling him/her to rewards — or liabilities — entitling him/her to costs. Inputs typically include any of the following: time, effort, loyalty, hard work, commitment, ability, adaptability, flexibility, tolerance, determination, enthusiasm, personal sacrifice, trust in superiors, support from co-workers and colleagues, and skill.

Outcomes are viewed as the positive and negative consequences which occur as a result of his/her relationship with another. When the ratio of inputs to outcomes is close, then an employee should have job satisfaction. Outcomes can be both tangible and intangible. Outcomes typically include any of the following: job security, salary, employee benefits, expenses, esteem, recognition, reputation, responsibility, sense of achievement, praise and thanks.

The comparisons and ratios are very subjective and are based on individual perceptions. After comparisons have been made, an individual may feel under-rewarded, equitably rewarded or over-rewarded. A feeling of equity will occur when the two ratios are equal. Equity theory suggests that employees are not only interested in rewards but also interested in *comparative* rewards. Such rewards, however, are best applied to *extrinsic* rewards, such as pay, promotion and benefits, rather than *intrinsic* rewards, such as personal achievement and responsibility, as the latter are personal to the individual and less capable of objective comparison.

Expectancy theory

Expectancy theory is based on the work of Victor Vroom in the 1960s and focuses on how employees perceive the relationships between:

- effort
- performance
- rewards.

Expectancy theory suggests that employees will be motivated to act only when they have a reasonable expectancy that their behaviour will lead to the outcomes they desire (Figure 7.3). Motivational strength therefore increases if there are positive expectations of work outcomes, that is, how much an employee wants something and how likely he or she thinks they are to achieve it. Expectancy theory emphasises the need for organisations to relate rewards directly to performance and to ensure that the rewards provided are the rewards deserved and wanted by the recipients.
Expectancy theory assumes that:

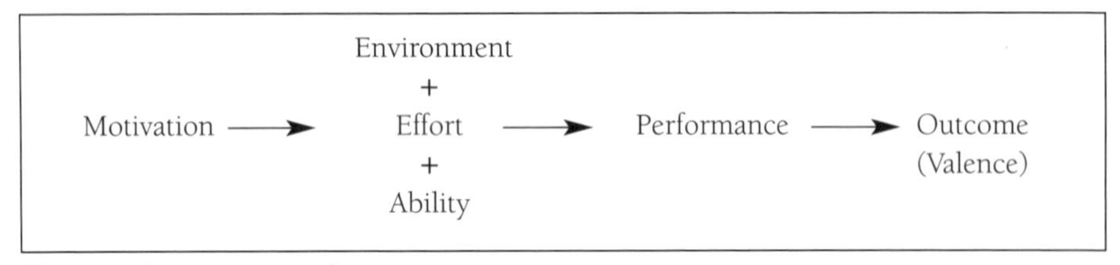

Figure 7.3 Expectancy theory

1. Behaviour is determined by a set of forces, both in the individual and in the work environment.
2. Employees choose to make decisions about their own performance in organisations depending on their own needs, desires and goals.
3. Employees make decisions regarding their behaviour according to their perceptions of the extent to which their behaviour might lead to desired outcomes.

Vroom concluded that performance leads to various outcomes, each of which has an associated value called its valence. **Valence** is the strength of belief in the likelihood of the occurrence of an associated attractive reward.

Vroom also classed rewards as *intrinsic* and *extrinsic*. Employees can exercise a degree of personal control over intrinsic rewards, for example, fulfilling higher-level personal needs and self-esteem. Extrinsic rewards, such as pay and other working conditions, are generally outside the control of an employee as these rewards are provided by the organisation. Rewards associated with intrinsic factors are more likely to produce job satisfaction.

Goal-setting theory

Goal-setting theory suggests that motivation is based on goals or objectives that employees set for themselves. Research by Locke (1968) confirmed that employee performance improved when employees set specific rather than vague goals. The research also found, given adequate levels of ability and commitment by employees, that more difficult goals tend to elicit greater performance than easier goals would. Goals, however, must not be so difficult that they are unattainable.

Goal-setting theory also suggests that the rate of acceptance of and commitment to particular goals will determine employee efforts in their attainment. Organisational support for employee goals together with employee performance should lead to both intrinsic and extrinsic rewards, which in turn should lead to employee satisfaction.

Reinforcement theory

This motivational process addresses why some behaviours are maintained over time and why other behaviours change. Reinforcement is defined as *any effect that causes behaviour to be repeated or inhibited*. When reinforcement theory is applied to motivation it is linked to learning. The reinforcement theory of motivation suggests that a given behaviour is a product of the consequences of earlier behaviour and proposes that behaviour resulting in positive rewards is likely to be repeated, whereas behaviour resulting in punishment is less likely to be repeated.

Positive reinforcement is a method of strengthening behaviour by providing a reward for a desired behaviour. **Punishment** discourages undesired behaviours by using negative outcomes or unpleasant consequences when undesired behaviour occurs.

Reinforcement theory is more concerned with controlling the behaviour of employees than with what or how behaviour is motivated. It concerns control and power over others, for example, when employees are to be controlled, and when managers set proper conditions to encourage high performance while discouraging negative activities.

7.4 The psychological contract

The relationship between employees and employers can be described in many ways. Any relationship is formed within a context of rights, expectations and obligations on the part of each party. Relationships are also influenced by the cultural norms of what is and what is not acceptable about the balance of power within the particular organisation. The balance between the employee and the organisation has been summed up in the phrase 'psychological contract'. The psychological contract is subjective, unwritten, and often not discussed or negotiated. A major feature of psychological contracts is the concept of mutuality — that there is a common and agreed understanding of promises and obligations that the respective parties have made to each other about work, pay, commitment, flexibility, security and career advancement.

The employee, for example, offers:

- loyalty
- conformity to requirements
- commitment to the employer's goals and trust in their employer not to abuse their goodwill.

In return, the employer offers:

- security of employment
- promotion prospects
- training and development
- flexibility.

The psychological contract underpins the work relationship by acting in a similar manner to that of Herzberg's hygiene factors. Good psychological contracts may not always result in superior performance, or indeed satisfied employees; but poor psychological contracts tend to act as demotivators, which can be reflected in lower levels of employee commitment, higher levels of absenteeism and turnover, and reduced performance.

The psychological contract between employers and employees in the past was a job for life in return for effort and loyalty. The new-style contract is lifelong employability in exchange for effort. The employer is offering development and experience which are valuable to employees in their current and future roles.

7.5 Key points

Motivation is a force that influences the behaviour of people. It is important for managers to have an understanding of what motivates employees as motivation, together with ability and environmental factors, determines employee performance. The key to effective work performance lies in an understanding of human motivation.

Overall, there are three motivational perspectives:

- content
- process
- reinforcement.

Content perspectives on motivation are concerned with whatever factors result in motivation. Some of the content theories include:

- Maslow's hierarchy of needs
- Alderfer's ERG model
- McClelland's achievement motivation
- Herzberg's two-factor theory
- McGregor's Theory X and Theory Y.

Process perspectives on motivation are concerned with how motivation occurs. Process perspectives include:

- equity theory
- expectancy theory
- goal-setting theory.

The *reinforcement* perspective on motivation is concerned with how motivation is maintained. It suggests that behaviour resulting in rewarding consequences is likely to be repeated, whereas behaviour resulting in negative consequences is less likely to be repeated.

It is important for managers to realise that there is no 'one best way' to motivate employees. Managers must take account of different situations, psychological variables and the behaviour of employees when motivating individuals. Managers are therefore advised to use a combination of approaches that best suit the circumstances.

Important terms and concepts

Alderfer's ERG model (p.106)
content theories of motivation (p.103)
empowerment (p.103)

equity theory (p.109)
expectancy theory (p.110)
goal-setting theory (p.111)
human relations approach (p.103)
human resource approach (p.103)
Herzberg's two-factor theory (p.107)
inputs (p.109)
Maslow's hierarchy of needs (p.104)
McClelland's achievement motivation (p.106)
McGregor's Theory X, Theory Y (p.108)
motivation defined (p.102)
outcomes (p.109)
participation (p.103)
positive reinforcement (p.111)
process theories of motivation (p.109)
psychological contract (p.112)
punishment (p.111)
reinforcement theory (p.111)
traditional approach (p.102)

Questions for review

1. Discuss Maslow's theory of needs and outline the relevance of this theory for employee motivation in modern organisations.
2. Identify and discuss various ways in which managers can attempt to increase the motivation of employees.
3. What are the differences between motivation and hygiene factors in the two-factor theory?
4. Write brief notes on:
   a. Equity theory
   b. Expectancy theory
   c. Goal-setting theory.
5. Summarise the motivation process.
6. Compare and contrast the content, process and reinforcement perspectives on motivation.
7. Discuss the implications for management of any two theories of motivation.

8
HUMAN RESOURCE MANAGEMENT

Objectives

This chapter will help you to:

- understand the background and the development of human resource management in organisations
- define human resource management
- identify human resource management activities performed by managers
- recognise the contribution of human resource management activities to the overall functioning of organisations.

8.1 Background to human resource management

During the 1890s, an increasing number of employers in Britain and North America accepted responsibility for the welfare of their employees. In Britain, organisations such as Cadbury and Rowntree appointed 'industrial welfare' workers, who were responsible for ensuring the well-being of women and children in the workforce and to watch over their health and behaviour. During the nineteenth century, conditions of work for most employees in factories were very poor. During this period also, the trade union movement was developing as individuals realised the strength they could gain by coming together to negotiate with employers.

Due to the lack of skilled labour during the First World War (1914–18), many women were encouraged to become part of the industrial workforce for the first time. This expanded the role of recruitment and selection functions within organisations and resulted in:

- greater concern for workers' welfare
- making the best possible use of employees.

During the 1920s and 1930s, internal organisational practices were influenced by developments in management theory, for example, scientific management and the human relations movement (see Chapter 1). In particular, the Hawthorne experiments highlighted the importance both of integrating employees into the organisation and the 'controlling' personnel function.

During the Second World War (1939–45), there was an increase in demand for materials and labour — particularly in the armed forces, auxiliary forces and the munitions industries — resulting in increased welfare functions, including the provision of training programmes to maximise labour productivity, and the improvement of morale and motivation.

During the Second World War, joint consultation between management and workforce was practised. There was also an increased emphasis on health and safety and the need for specialists to deal with industrial relations. This resulted in the welfare worker (now to be known as personnel manager, as the term 'welfare' was viewed more as a feminine issue among the increasing number of male employees) becoming the spokesperson for management in discussions with trade unions. This could be regarded as the beginning of the industrial relations function as performed by modern-day human resource managers.

During the 1960s and 1970s, there was a growth in the amount of employment legislation that reinforced the importance of personnel officers in areas such as pay negotiations and dealing with trade unions. During the late 1980s, the term 'human resource management' emerged in Britain.

Traditionally, a personnel department was often perceived as an administrative support function with a lowly status. More recently, personnel has become very much part of an organisation's human resource management, and human resource management is conceived to be more than personnel and to have a wider range than the core personnel function. In order for human resource management to be strategic it had to encompass all the human resource areas of the organisation and to be engaged with by all employees. In addition, decentralisation and devolvement of responsibility are also seen as very much part of the human resource management strategy as it facilitates communication, involvement and commitment of middle management and other employees within the organisation.

8.2 Human resource management (HRM) defined

Defining human resource management is still a controversial activity. For some researchers, human resource management is a new approach to managing the labour process. For others human resource management is simply a relabelling of personnel management and is viewed as 'old wine in new bottles'.

Human resource management has been defined (Bratton and Gold 2003) as:

> That part of the management process that specialises in the management of people in work organisations. HRM emphasises that

> employees are critical to achieving sustainable competitive advantage, that human resources practices need to be integrated with the corporate strategy, and that human resource specialists help organisational controllers to meet both efficiency and equity objectives.

From this definition, individuals in organisations are 'human resources', implying that the management of people is comparable to the management of other organisational resources. More than other resources, however, it is the individuals or the people who make the major difference to an organisation. The human resources also differ from other resources in organisations because individuals have the ability to question and evaluate the actions of management. Employees may also form groups and trade unions to strengthen their positions in organisations.

There has been considerable debate and discussion in management literature comparing human resource management with traditional personnel management. Researchers agree that while similarities exist between personnel management and human resource management, there are some key characteristics which differentiate traditional personnel management from human resource management:

- HRM is integrated into strategic planning, as organisations realise that competitive advantage can be achieved through managing people as efficiently and effectively as other resources.
- HRM emphasises the importance of leadership in creating 'vision', innovation and employee commitment at all levels of the organisation.
- With HRM, the role of line managers (supervisors) is increased, for example, tasks traditionally undertaken by personnel management are often devolved to line management.
- HRM policies, such as recruitment, selection, reward and employee relations are fully integrated and consistent with an organisation's culture.

Allowing for the problems of definitions and demarcation lines between various conceptions of human resource management, HRM has become a fashionable concept and a controversial subject since the 1980s, with its boundaries very much overlapping the traditional areas of personnel management, industrial relations, organisational behaviour, and strategic and operational management. Many proponents of HRM argue that it addresses the centrality of employees in the organisation, and that their motivation and commitment to organisational goals need to be nurtured. While this is by no means a new concept, the HRM perspective would suggest that a range of organisational objectives have been arranged in a strategic way to enhance the performance of employees in achieving these goals.

8.3 Hard and soft HRM

Legge's (1995) review of the literature on personnel and human resource management identified problems with 'hard' and 'soft' human resource management.

Hard HRM emphasises the term *resource* and views people as another economic factor and a cost that must be controlled. The business needs of the organisation suggest that human resources will be acquired, used and dispensed as corporate planning requires. Hard HRM pays little attention to the needs of those human resources.

Hard HRM is sometimes defined in terms of the particular policies that stress a cost-minimisation strategy with an emphasis on leanness in production and the use of labour as a resource in the employment relationship.

Soft HRM focuses on the term *human* and emphasises the importance of training and development, enabling better skilled employees to give a competitive advantage to their organisation. The human aspects also suggest that all employees (regardless of grade) should be developed and that the behavioural aspects of people at work should be considered to be of the utmost importance.

Soft HRM also views the employee as being integrated to a work process that values trust, commitment and communication.

8.4 Human resource management activities

The objective of an organisation's human resource management strategy is to maximise the return on investment from an organisation's human capital and minimise financial risk. Human resource managers seek to achieve this by aligning the supply of skilled and qualified individuals, and the capabilities of the current workforce, with the ongoing and future business plans and requirements of the organisation in order to maximise return on investment. Human resource management activities vary from one organisation to another and are affected by the size and structure of an organisation. In general, the activities performed by a human resource manager may be divided into the following areas:

- staffing
- employee development
- employee relations
- rewards
- employee maintenance
- performance management.

Staffing

Traditionally, human resource managers spent a great deal of time recruiting and selecting employees. Up to recently, however, the employment situation had shifted from an employers' to an employees' market. As a consequence, there was a shift in the proportion of employees in full-time permanent employment towards more flexible arrangements including self-employment. Employment patterns are changing, and changing work methods give rise to requirements for different and new skills and for existing employees to be more flexible in adapting to new working methods. Hiring staff on an *ad hoc* basis puts the continuity and development of all employees at risk. The recruitment, selection and promotion of employees are expensive processes and are often difficult to reverse if errors are made.

To deal with these variables, **human resource planning** is needed to analyse current employee needs and to prepare an organisation for future requirements. One of the primary functions of human resource planning is to estimate what numbers of people and what skills are required to achieve organisational goals. A human resource plan should present a detailed analysis of staffing requirements for an organisation and should include a statement on how vacancies are to be filled. Human resource planning, therefore, is the starting point for establishing an organisation's human resource strategy, as this planning seeks to integrate the operations of an organisation with the skills of a labour force in order to satisfy customer demands.

Human resource planning addresses issues such as:

- *Accommodation* — Is there a need for more or fewer rooms, desks, etc?
- *Costs* — Where is there a need for additional/fewer resources?
- *Culture* — How are changes going to affect the way people interact?
- *Development* — Will there be different opportunities for staff development?
- *Industrial relations* — How will trade unions react to changes?
- *Organisation development* — Do reporting relationships need to be changed or reorganised?
- *Promotion* — What opportunities for individual advancement will there be?
- *Recruitment* — What number and sort of people will need to be recruited?
- *Redundancy* — Which groups are likely to face redundancy and how is this going to be dealt with?
- *Reward systems* — Should financial and non-financial rewards be revised?
- *Training and retraining* — Which groups need to develop new skills?

- *Working practices* — Is there a need to rethink the ways in which tasks are addressed?

A human resource plan illustrates the number of employees that an organisation will need for the next stage in the staffing function — the recruitment process.

The recruitment process

The major stages of the recruitment process are:
- job analysis, job descriptions and person specifications
- advertising
- administration of recruitment.

Job analysis consists of data about each job, what activities are to be performed and what skills are needed. Job analysis will often involve the use of job descriptions (Figure 8.1) and person specifications (Figure 8.2).

Job descriptions — usually include the following elements:
- job title
- rates of pay
- grade
- location
- department
- job summary — a brief statement of why the job exists
- job content — a list of the main duties to be performed
- reporting structure
- miscellaneous, for example, shift-work and car allowance.

Job title:	Human Resources Manager
Department:	Human Resources
Reports to:	Chief Executive Officer
Responsible for:	Employees in all departments
Main duties:	Recruitment, selection, training, development, industrial relations, rewards, health, safety, welfare

Figure 8.1 Job description (sample)

Person specifications outline the knowledge, skills and personal qualities a person will require in order to be able to perform the tasks outlined in a job description. The following elements are commonly included in person specifications:

- physical make-up — any necessary and justifiable (that is, non-discriminatory in equality/legislation terms) physical requirements which are essential to the job
- qualifications, education, training and experience
- personal qualities, for example, good communication, written and oral skills, confidence, dependability
- motivation, such as high expectations of self and others.

Job Title:	Human Resources Manager
Department:	Human Resources Department
Qualifications:	Graduate in relevant subject
Experience:	Minimum of two years' experience in a unionised environment
Knowledge and skills:	Knowledge and skills in employee relations and legislation, computer skills, organisational skills
Personal qualities:	Good communication, confidence, dependability

Figure 8.2 Person specification (sample)

Administration of recruitment

Recruitment is the business of attracting sufficient suitable candidates for the job at a reasonable cost. The administration of the recruitment process is usually done by the personnel/HRM department. This involves placing advertisements, sending application forms and job descriptions to potential candidates, and receiving the completed forms. The advantage of the personnel/HRM department in dealing with the administration of recruitment is that consistency between departments can exist, with a corporate approach for differing posts. There are various methods of recruiting people, these include:

- internal advertising
- newspaper advertisements
- radio, TV and cinema
- word of mouth
- local schools, colleges and universities
- recruitment consultants
- recruitment fairs
- Internet
- specialist and professional papers and journals

- job centres
- headhunting.

The best method is the one that produces the most suitable candidates within reasonable cost restraints.

The selection process

Once an organisation's advertisement has attracted a manageable number of suitably qualified and/or experienced individuals, the human resource manager must decide on the best way to select interested candidates. Among the selection methods available to managers are:

- Application forms provide the basic information needed for an initial trawl prior to short-listing. The forms need to be designed for easy use, with the opportunity for individuals to offer additional material where they want.
- Curricula vitae (CVs) are similar to application forms, except that the candidates select their own ways of presenting the data about themselves and their careers.
- Interviews remain popular because they offer an opportunity for face-to-face conversation. They also allow for comparison between candidates.
- Tests, for example, aptitude, personality and selection tests, which relate to the skills necessary to do the job. It is important that a prescribed test really does test the skills that are needed to do the job and does not discriminate unfairly.
- Assessment centres (assessment of several candidates together by several observers using a variety of selection methods, for example, psychological tests, team-building exercises, structured discussions and role-playing exercises). The value lies in the variety of evidence collected; but assessment centres are expensive to run, both in time and money, so are usually reserved for senior appointments such as chief executives.

The ultimate goal of selection is often expressed as *choosing the best person for the job*. The objectives of the selection process, therefore, are to:

- gather as much relevant information as possible
- assess each candidate in order to forecast performance on the job
- give information to applicants so that they can judge whether or not they would wish to accept an offer of employment.

An organisation may decide to use a variety of selection methods, for example, supplementing interviews with psychological tests and personality questionnaires, depending on the vacancy to be filled.

Employee development

A definition of employee development is:

> The skilful provision and organisation of learning experiences in the workplace so that performance can be improved, work goals can be achieved, and that — through enhancing the skills, knowledge, learning ability and enthusiasm at every level — there can be continuous organisational as well as individual growth. Employee development must, therefore, be part of a wider strategy for the business, aligned with the organisation's corporate mission and goals (Harrison 2000).

Employee development relates to employees acquiring a broad range of skills through planned activities and experience, and is concerned with an individual's overall career development rather than training for his/her current role.

To support staff development, the human resource manager engages in:

- analysing training requirements
- appraising employee performance
- developing employee career plans
- encouraging employee involvement
- providing development opportunities
- providing employee counselling
- improving employee welfare.

Individual employees may attend management courses, participate in job rotation, committees and special projects, or train as understudies of various senior managers.

The human resource manager needs to assess the type of training that will benefit the organisation as well as each individual employee. Training and development may be conducted on the job, for example, job instruction, coaching, job rotation, and participation in special projects and assignments. Alternatively, off-the-job training may be used, for example, seminar/workshop attendance, role-playing and guided reading.

Appraising employee performance is another mechanism for employee development as it concerns making judgments about past performance of employees. Employee appraisals can be used to improve current performance by providing feedback on strengths and weaknesses. Performance appraisals should be linked to a performance improvement process, which can be used to identify training needs and to focus on career plans and career development. Appraisals can be effective for increasing employee motivation which, in turn, increases organisational performance. The performance appraisal interview provides time for an employee and manager to discuss an employee's progress in his or her current position, as well as discussing opportunities for progression within the organisation.

A concern for employee welfare is also a function of the human resource manager. This function includes:

- ensuring that health and safety legislation is enforced
- maintaining good employee relations
- providing counselling (that is, helping people to help themselves)
- providing an employee assistance programme (EAP).

Many types of issues can be dealt with by an EAP, for example, alcohol abuse, verbal abuse, racial harassment, retirement, marital problems, disability, gambling, bereavement, financial advice, literacy, AIDS and other medical issues, redundancy, legal matters, and divorce (Berridge and Cooper 1994).

If employee development is successfully designed and managed, it can contribute to the success of the organisation within the contemporary business environment.

Performance management

Armstrong and Baron (2004) define performance management as:

> A process which contributes to the effective management of individuals and teams in order to achieve high levels of organisational performance. As such, it establishes shared understanding about what is to be achieved and an approach to leading and developing people which will ensure that it is achieved.

Performance management is an established way of providing feedback, guidance and monitoring for employees. The assessment process in performance management is linked to job definitions and is rigorous and objective. It is based on organisational objective-setting and individual development plans and it is sometimes linked with financial rewards. For many systems, an element of self-appraisal is also included. Some of the reasons why managers might want to appraise their staff include:

- *Human resource considerations* — to ensure that the abilities and energies of employees are being used effectively. Managers would hope to find out more about their employees and to make better use of each individual's talents and expertise.
- *Training* — to identify training needs for new tasks and to improve poor performance among employees.

- *Promotion* — talking to employees about their aspirations as well as finding out about their performance can assist decision-making about who is ready for promotion.
- *Planning* — to identify skill shortages and succession needs.

Performance management is usually taken to mean an increased emphasis on specifying what is wanted and rewarding those employees who are able to deliver it satisfactorily.

Employee relations

The term employee relations was conceived as a replacement for the term industrial relations. Employee relations includes negotiations between management and union representatives (in a union environment) and dealing with disciplinary procedures and grievances. In any organisation, there will be occasions when problems or difficulties occur between management and employees. In order that these problems do not turn into bigger issues, suitable ways of dealing with them are devised to resolve them.

If a problem arises from a particular activity, or inactivity, of management, this may result in an employee having a grievance. **Grievance procedures** exist to enable employees to have formal means of complaint about their employment terms and conditions, working environment, and related issues.

If a problem arises from the behaviour or attitude of an employee, disciplinary action may be called for. **Disciplinary rules** set the standards of workplace behaviour. Generally, these rules refer to overall conduct, health and safety, security, time-keeping, and attendance. Disciplinary rules help to ensure a consistent and fair approach to the treatment of employees.

Breaches of disciplinary rules vary in their seriousness; for example, a minor infringement, such as occasional late arrival at work, might merit an oral warning which might not be formally recorded, whereas more serious infringements might prompt written warnings. Gross misconduct can result in dismissal, for example, because of theft or drug misuse in the workplace.

In a unionised environment, trade unions pursue a common interest with management in promoting standards of conduct by all. By representing their members, their role is to promote and protect their members' rights.

The ability to manage conflict remains a key issue for many organisations. **Mediation** as a method or technique of resolving workplace issues represents an important shift from the traditional industrial relations framework, with its emphasis on formal discipline and grievance procedures, towards more of a 'win-win' approach consistent with the philosophy of human resource management.

Rewards

Human resource managers design and administer appropriate reward systems, evaluate jobs, decide on benefits and provide fair treatment for all employees. There are a number of words which are used to describe what an employee receives in return for his/her work efforts. These words include:

- *Benefits* — the non-cash elements of an employee's reward package, for example, a paid holiday.
- *Compensation* — payment for work performed, injuries received or loss of employment (i.e. pay and benefits).
- *Salary* — a financial reward for work done and usually received on a monthly basis.
- *Wages* — a financial reward for work done and usually received on a weekly basis (generally associated with manual workers).

Reward packages can include financial and non-financial rewards:

- employee share options
- payments for medical insurance and pensions
- childcare
- assistance for further education
- company cars.

An effective reward system has four main characteristics:

- The reward system must meet the needs of the employee for basic necessities. These needs include the physiological and security needs identified by Maslow and the hygiene factors identified by Herzberg.
- The rewards should compare favourably with those offered by other organisations. Unfavourable comparisons with people in other settings could result in feelings of inequity.
- The distribution of rewards within the organisation must be equitable. When some employees believe they are underpaid in comparison with others in the organisation, the probable results are low morale and poor performance.
- The reward system must recognise that different people have different needs and that people choose different paths to satisfy those needs. Insofar as possible, a variety of rewards and a variety of methods for satisfying needs should be made available to employees.

Marchington and Wilkinson (2000) suggest that employers need to turn their attention to non-financial rewards in the form of recognition, appreciation and feedback for their employees. Other valuable non-financial rewards are job-design initiatives to make work more satisfying and fulfilling, and the provision of variety, involvement, autonomy and responsibility.

Given the large cost to an organisation of reward packages, it is important that managers assess the benefit that accrues to the organisation because of those packages. An organisation must provide reasonable pay and appropriate benefits to its employees; however, it is in the best interest of the organisation that its resources are managed wisely. As part of the recruiting process, it is necessary for the organisation to be seen as an attractive employer in order to hire high-quality human resources. The attractiveness of an organisation as an employer is a function, in part, of the total compensation package, which includes employee benefits.

Employee maintenance

Employee maintenance includes the provision of equal opportunities, the monitoring of workplace health and safety policies, and staff retention endeavours. Human resource managers need to be familiar with legislation and their organisation's policies in relation to women, disabled people, ethnic minorities and other sectors.

Health and safety policies are now statutory requirements for all employers. According to the Safety, Health and Welfare at Work Acts (2005) employers are primarily responsible for creating and maintaining a safe and healthy workplace. The main items covered under health and safety legislation include:

- arrangements for emergencies
- safety provision
- reporting of incidents and injuries
- recording of accidents
- the provision and use of safe working equipment.

Human resource managers and employers should be familiar with current employment law in order to fulfil their legal obligations to employees and be clear about their own rights.

8.5 Key points

The concept of human resource management and the use of the term grew and developed during the 1980s and 1990s. Its conceptual origin can be traced back to the 1890s when the human resource manager or personnel practitioner was involved with welfare work. Human resource management differs from traditional personnel management activities as it is concerned with the *integration of employees* in all departments of an organisation working towards the achievement of common goals. Human resource management also takes a *strategic perspective* on recruiting and developing employees and emphasises the importance of the manager as leader, together with devolving and delegating power to supervisors (line managers).

The activities of human resource managers have now shifted from the original narrower focus of welfare work to issues related to the acquisition, development and maintainance of human resources in an organisation. Human resource management activities vary depending on the size, structure and culture of an organisation. There are, however, a number of activities common to all organisations, including:

- human resource planning
- recruitment and selection of employees
- managing employee relations
- rewarding employees
- employee development
- retaining employees.

Human resource managers in Ireland cannot ignore the pace of change and its effect on employers and employees, such as the skills shortages in evidence today. Human resource managers need to anticipate such changes and to carefully plan, recruit and select employees, and develop methods of retaining their most valuable assets — their human resources.

Important terms and concepts

employee development (p.123)
employee maintenance (p.127)
employee relations (p.125)
hard HRM (p.118)
HRM defined (p.116)
human resource planning (p.119)
job analysis (p.120)
job description (p.120)
mediation (p.125)
performance management (p.124)
person specification (p.120)
recruitment process (p.120)
rewards (p.126)
selection process (p.122)
soft HRM (p.118)
staffing (p.119)

Questions for review

1. Describe the main functions performed by human resource managers in organisations.

2. Trace the development of human resource management from personnel management.

3. Evaluate the contribution of the human resource manager to the success of an organisation.

4. Describe the recruitment and selection process in an organisation.

5. Discuss organisational rewards in the context of some of the motivational theories with which you are familiar.

9
STRATEGIC MANAGEMENT

Objectives

This chapter will help you to:

- recognise the steps in a strategic management process
- identify various levels of strategy
- understand portfolio management techniques
- explain strategic human resource management.

9.1 Strategy defined

Strategy can be defined as an action plan for the future to accomplish organisational goals. An action plan should address questions such as what to do and how to do it. Strategy is a planning activity that top managers perform to provide long-term direction and scope to an organisation (see Chapter 3). Strategy also achieves *advantage* for the organisation by its uses of *resources* within a changing *environment*. Porter (1996) states that an essential element of strategy is choosing what *not* to do, which is as important as choosing what to do.

Strategic management as a discipline originated in the 1950s and 1960s. Prior to this time the various functions of management were separate with little overall co-ordination or strategy. Strategic management is a way of approaching business opportunities and challenges, and is a comprehensive and ongoing management process aimed at formulating and implementing effective strategies (Griffin 2008). Strategic management includes the maintenance of a 'vision of the future' that is constantly updated by data on both internal and external environments (Aktouf 1996). At its simplest, strategic management can be described as a plan of action that enables an organisation to move from where it is now to where it wants to be in the future.

Strategic management, therefore, is an ongoing process influenced by:

- senior management
- input from line managers
- the environment
- resources.

Strategic management is concerned with complexity arising out of ambiguous and non-routine situations with organisational-wide rather than operational-wide implications. Strategic management also involves making strategic choices for the future and turning strategy into action. **Strategic management** differs in nature and scope from operational management because of its:

- ambiguous/uncertain nature
- complexity
- organisation-wide focus
- long-term implications.

Operational management is:

- routinised
- operationally specific
- short-term.

In general, a well-conceived strategy addresses three areas:

- *Distinctive competence* — something the organisation does exceptionally well.
- *Scope* — the part of a strategy that specifies the range of markets in which an organisation will compete.
- *Resource deployment* — how an organisation distributes its resources across the areas in which it competes.

9.2 The strategic management process

The strategic management process may be divided into five steps.

Step 1: Organisational direction

The first step in the strategic management process begins with senior managers evaluating an organisation's position in relation to the organisation's *mission* and *goals*. As described in Chapter 3, a mission is an organisation's reason for existing and indicates the future direction that senior management has for the organisation. A goal is a desired future state that the organisation attempts to realise (Daft 1998).

Objectives are clear and explicit and there is careful and thorough analysis of the internal and external factors that might affect its strategic direction. The structure of the organisation should be suited to the strategy to be followed; and the various control systems, such as budgets and management by objectives, should facilitate organisational direction. These controls provide means by which senior management can assess if people in the organisation are meeting expected objectives and if the strategic direction of the organisation is being attained.

While a sense of direction is important, it can also stifle creativity, especially if it is rigidly enforced. In an uncertain and ambiguous world, fluidity can be more important than a finely tuned strategy. When a strategy becomes internalised into a corporate culture, it can lead to groupthink. It can also cause an organisation to define itself too narrowly.

Step 2: Environmental analysis

Environmental analysis involves looking at the internal *strengths* and *weaknesses* of an organisation together with the *opportunities* and *threats* posed by the *external* environment.

This is often referred to as a **SWOT analysis**. SWOT stands for:

- strengths
- weaknesses
- opportunities
- threats.

Strengths and weaknesses — *internal environmental analysis* — tend to concentrate on the present and past; opportunities and threats — *external environmental analysis* — usually refer to the present and future of an organisation.

Organisational strengths are skills and capabilities that enable an organisation to conceive and implement its strategies. A **distinctive competence** is a strength possessed by an organisation. A main purpose of SWOT analysis is to discover an organisation's distinctive competences so that the organisation can choose and implement strategies that exploit its unique organisational strengths.

Organisational weaknesses are skills and capabilities that do not enable an organisation to choose and implement strategies that support its objectives. An organisation has essentially two ways of addressing weaknesses. First, it may need to make investments to obtain the strengths required to implement strategies that support its mission. Second, the organisation may need to modify its mission so that it can be accomplished with the skills and capabilities that the organisation already possesses.

Organisational opportunities are areas in the environment that, if exploited, may generate high performance.

Organisational threats are areas in the environment that increase the difficulty for an organisation in achieving high performance.

Step 3: Strategy formulation

Strategy formulation involves senior managers *gathering relevant information to determine future actions of an organisation*. This process suggests that, from a SWOT analysis (Step 2), managers have to make decisions or *strategic choices* to enable their organisation to meet its goals. Strategies are formulated at corporate (top), business (middle) and functional (lower) levels (see 9.3 Levels of strategy).

There is no one right way in which strategy is formulated, for example, strategies which are formulated in a fast-changing environment are not likely to be the same as in an environment in which there is little change. Typically, strategy formulation is written about as though it is developed by managers in an intended, planned fashion. **Intended strategy** is an expression of desired strategic direction deliberately formulated or planned by managers.

Often organisations use an **emergent strategy** — a pattern of action that develops over time from within the organisation rather than from the top down. Strategy *emerges* from innovation and from the variety and diversity which exist in and around organisations. New ideas, and therefore innovation, may come from anywhere in an organisation or from the world around it.

Step 4: Strategy implementation

Strategy implementation involves *the activities that are required to put strategies into action*. It focuses on the processes through which strategies are achieved, for example, structure, leadership and control systems. This step focuses on *how* the strategy is to be achieved.

In many organisations, however, the attempt to follow detailed intended strategies is only partially achieved in practice. The intended strategy is, therefore, replaced by a realised strategy. A **realised strategy** is the strategy actually being followed by an organisation in practice. There are various reasons for this, such as: the plans are unworkable; the environment changes after the strategy has been drawn up and the managers decide that the strategy, as planned, should not be put into effect; or people in the organisation or influential stakeholders do not go along with the strategies.

Step 5: Strategy evaluation

Strategy evaluation determines whether *actual* change and performance is taking place and whether or not the change matches the *desired* change and performance.

9.3 Levels of strategy

Strategy is generally formulated at three levels:

- corporate
- business
- functional.

Corporate-level strategy

Corporate-level strategy describes an organisation's overall direction. It is concerned with the question *What business should we be in?* It considers the combination of businesses in terms of markets, products and nations. In the case of large organisations, it looks at the management of its various business units. A strategic business unit (SBU) is a unit of a company that has a separate mission and separate objectives, and can be planned independently from other company businesses (see Chapter 5). Large organisations develop separate business-level strategies for each of their divisions or units, each of which might be engaged in producing very different products or services. In the case of smaller organisations, corporate and business-level strategies may be combined.

Corporate-level strategy may be viewed as a grand plan for an organisation which describes the general actions to be taken to achieve long-term objectives. A grand strategy represents the overall direction a business intends to follow. Senior managers may choose from three grand strategy options (Table 9.1):

- retrenchment
- stability
- growth.

Grand strategy	*Characteristics*	*Reason for implementation*
Retrenchment	Cutting back on range of products or markets	Management recognises that its organisation is performing badly.
Stability	Continuing with the same products and markets	Management recognises that its organisation is performing well and opts for low risk and little change in a stable environment.
Growth	Seeking to add new products and new markets	Management wants its organisation to perform much better, preferring high risk and change.

Table 9.1 Grand strategy alternatives

A **retrenchment strategy** is implemented by an organisation if senior management decides to reduce an organisation's size in terms of employees, production or assets. This may be the result of a decline in demand for an organisation's products, the introduction of new technology or from increased competition. Retrenchment usually involves selling off parts of a business or even the liquidation of an entire organisation.

A **stability strategy** involves an organisation's attempt to remain the same size or to grow in a very slow controlled way. This strategy may be implemented after a period of rapid growth in order to 'take stock' and ensure that the expansion is viable.

A **growth strategy** involves an organisation developing its market position, through increased investment, new product development and diversification into new markets, for example, foreign markets, to encourage expansion.

Business-level strategy

Business-level strategy is concerned with the question *How do we succeed in this particular business?* Porter (1980) proposed three business strategies known as Porter's generic strategies (see Chapter 2). A second classification of business-level strategy was developed by Miles and Snow (1978). These authors suggested that a business-level strategy can usually be identified with one of four categories (Table 9.2):

- defender strategies
- prospector strategies
- analyser strategies
- reactor strategies.

Strategy	*Definition*	*Example*
Defender	Focuses on existing customers, maintains stable growth	Corner shops
Prospector	Focuses on innovation and growth, encourages risk taking	Computer software suppliers
Analyser	Focuses on maintaining current markets with moderate innovation in new markets	Major breweries
Reactor	No clear strategy, reacts to changes in the environment	Street vendors

Table 9.2 Miles and Snow's business strategies

According to Miles and Snow, an organisation that implements a **defender strategy** has a limited product line and its management focus is on improving the efficiency of existing operations. This strategy concentrates on protecting current market share, maintaining stable growth and serving current customers.

An organisation that implements a **prospector strategy** focuses on new product development, innovation and market opportunities and typically has a number of product lines. Such an organisation would be constantly expanding into new markets and would also be a high risk taker.

An organisation that implements an **analyser strategy** generally operates in at least two different markets, one stable (thus protecting existing operations) and one variable (thus creating new market opportunities). Managers in these organisations emphasise efficiency in the stable market and innovation in the variable market.

An organisation that implements a **reactor strategy** has no consistent strategic approach. Such a company fails to anticipate environmental changes and usually responds to these changes only in a piecemeal fashion.

Functional-level strategy

Functional-level strategy is concerned with the ongoing functional operations of an organisation. The functions represented in an organisation depend on the type of business, its size and its structure, but may include marketing, sales, research and development, finance and human resources. Strategy at the functional level addresses the question *How do we support the business-level competitive strategy?* All these functions need to follow the strategic plans of an organisation and must be integrated to ensure the overall success of an organisation.

9.4 The corporate portfolio

Every organisation consists of at least one and usually many more products and services. These products or services represent the *business portfolio*; for example, in the car manufacturing industry there are various models of cars produced by each manufacturer. An organisation can be regarded as a 'portfolio' of businesses which managers balance by expanding investment in some while reducing investment in others. Managers have to decide on the investment of resources in their various businesses. Most organisations like to have a balanced mix of business units which are at different stages in their life cycles.

Portfolio management techniques are methods that organisations with many business units use to determine which businesses to engage in and how to manage these businesses in order to maximise corporate performance. Two well-known portfolio management techniques are:

- the Boston Consulting Group matrix
- the General Electric Business Screen.

The Boston Consulting Group (BCG) matrix

The use of the BCG matrix helps managers to define:

- What business should we be in?
- What is our basic mission?
- How should we allocate corporate resources across the various business units?

The matrix analyses businesses along two dimensions:

- business growth
- market share.

The business growth dimension measures how rapidly a whole industry is increasing in size, while market share measures the share a business unit has of this market in comparison to its competitors' share. By assessing each strategic business unit (SBU) on the basis of its market growth rate and relative market share, managers can make decisions about committing further financial resources to an SBU or, instead, to sell or liquidate an SBU.

Once managers have determined the growth rate of a market and the particular product or service market share, it is then possible to allocate each business unit to one of four quadrants in the matrix (see Figure 9.1). The allocation of individual business units to a particular position on the matrix should help managers to define strategic plans for a business, consistent with corporate strategy. The matrix classifies the types of business that a diversified organisation can engage in; in this case, dogs, cash cows, question marks and stars.

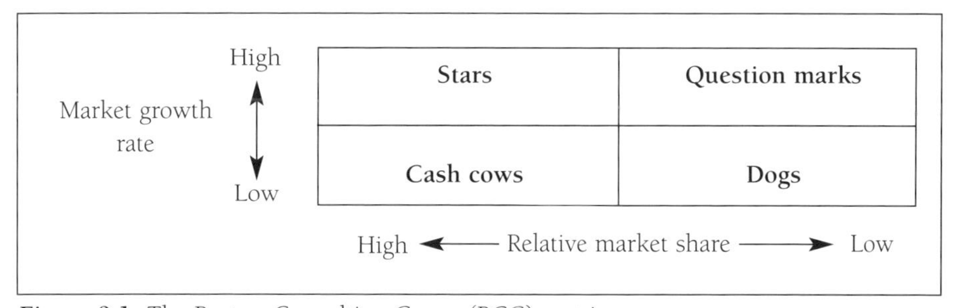

Figure 9.1 The Boston Consulting Group (BCG) matrix

Organisations may want to have a number of business units in each quadrant, with a number of products and services producing a cash flow among other businesses requiring an injection of cash.

Stars, according to the BCG matrix, are businesses that have the largest share of a rapidly growing market. Cash generated by cash cows should be invested in stars as they represent the best opportunities for future growth and survival. Stars are important because, as well as being successful, they have potential for further expansion. As a star's industry becomes more mature and growth slows, less investment will be required and the star will transform itself into a cash cow.

Question marks are businesses that have only a small share of a quickly growing market. The future performance of these particular businesses is uncertain and risky. The BCG matrix suggests that organisations should carefully invest in question marks. Investment might develop some into stars, while other question marks may fail regardless of investment. The BCG matrix suggests that an organisation should have some question marks in its portfolio as potential future stars.

Cash cows are businesses that have a large share of a market that is not expected to grow substantially. These businesses generate high profits and the excess cash they produce may be used for investment in question marks and stars. Low investment in cash cows means that these businesses should be profitable and they should also generate surplus cash as they age. From the corporate point of view, cash cows can be 'milked' to provide funds for investment in newer riskier businesses.

Dogs are businesses that have a very small share of a market that is not expected to grow. Dogs represent weak businesses and the BCG matrix suggests that organisations should not invest in these businesses or should consider selling them.

The BCG matrix has been criticised because of the difficulty in using it to describe some products or services and business units accurately; for example, the marginal difference between investing in a question mark with potential for growth and development of a star may be very small. It may be based on an estimation of market growth and the potential for future growth. Another criticism of the matrix is that it may be too narrowly focused, for example, other factors besides market growth and market share can determine the performance of a business. Despite its weaknesses, however, the portfolio concept still exists in organisations but it tends to help debate rather than prescribe what organisations should do.

The General Electric (GE) Business Screen

The GE Business Screen is another method of evaluating businesses along two dimensions:

- industry attractiveness
- competitive position.

Industry attractiveness and competitive position are used to classify businesses as winners, question marks, average businesses, losers or profit producers. The GE Business Screen suggests that several factors combine to determine a business's competitive position and the attractiveness of its industry (see Figure 9.2).

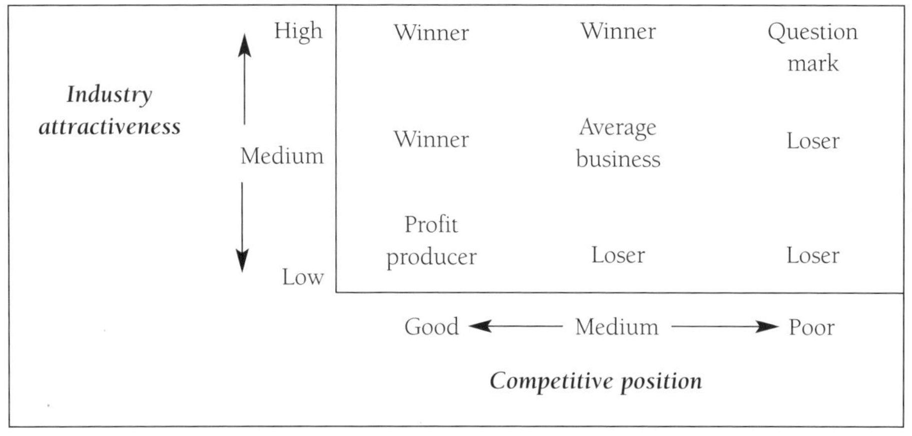

Figure 9.2 The General Electric (GE) Business Screen

Source: Hofer and Schendel 1978

Griffin (2008) suggests that **competitive position** is determined by:

- market share
- technological know-how
- product quality
- service network
- price competitiveness
- operating costs.

Griffin also suggests that **industry attractiveness** is determined by factors such as:

- market growth
- market size
- capital requirements
- competitive intensity.

According to the GE Business Screen, organisations should invest in winners and question marks, maintain the market position of average businesses and profit producers and sell losers.

9.5 Strategic human resource management

Strategic human resource management is a general approach to the strategic management of human resources in line with the intended future direction of an organisation. It is concerned with longer-term people issues and macro-concerns about structure, quality, culture, values, commitment and matching resources to future need. Strategic human resource management focuses on the link or *vertical integration* between human resource practices and an organisation's business strategy in order to enhance performance. Vertical integration can be demonstrated through the linking of a business goal to individual objective-setting and to the measurement and rewarding of that business goal. It also focuses on the relationship between best-practice or high-commitment human resource practices and organisational performance. The contribution that human resources may make to an organisation's performance and effectiveness has been linked to changes in the business environment, with the impact of globalisation leading to the need for increased competitiveness, flexibility, responsiveness, quality and the need for all functions of the business to demonstrate their contribution to the bottom line. Strategic human resource management is, therefore, concerned with explaining how human resource management influences organisational performance.

According to Beer *et al.* (1984), an organisation needs to establish a 'close fit' between its external business strategy and the elements of its internal human resource strategy. Similarly, Guest (1987) suggests that if the human resources component is not an integral part of the strategic planning process, the implementations of strategic business plans become more problematic:

> Because they are the most variable, and the least easy to understand and control of all management resources, effective utilisation of human resources is likely to give organisations a significant competitive advantage. The human resource dimension must therefore be fully integrated into the strategic planning process.

In order for organisations to gain a *competitive advantage* through their employees, human resource management must not be viewed as a stand-alone corporate issue but must be integrated with corporate strategy. Appropriate human resources are needed to implement strategies for an organisation to gain a competitive advantage through its human resources. Organisations, realising that their other resources may be easily imitated by competitors, might rely on their particular culture or teamworking situation, which may be more difficult to imitate, in order to gain competitive advantage.

According to Bratton and Gold (2003), an alignment between business strategy and human resource management strategy will improve organisational performance and competitiveness. They suggest that improved organisational performance results from policies of empowerment, team-working, workplace learning and employee commitment. Commitment to organisational competitiveness, as well as benefiting an organisation, also benefits employees by enhancing their perceptions of their own dignity, self-worth and identity.

Guest *et al.* (1997) suggest that innovation is a necessary part of any effective strategy for organisational success. Herriot and Pemberton (1997) note that a number of human requirements are needed for the successful pursuit of a strategy of innovation, including:

- access to adequate resources
- security
- autonomy (individuals being able to make decisions about how their own work gets done)
- teamworking.

Overall, therefore, strategic human resource management is differentiated from human resource management in a number of ways, particularly in its movement away from a micro-perspective on individual human resource functional areas to the adoption of a macro-perspective with its subsequent emphasis on vertical integration. It becomes apparent that the meaning of strategic human resource management tends to lie in the context of organisational performance, although organisational performance can be interpreted and measured in a variety of ways. These may range from delivering efficiency and flexibility through cost-reduction-driven strategies, to delivering employee commitment to organisational goals, to viewing human resources as a source of human capital and sustainable competitive advantage and a core business competence and key strategic asset.

9.6 Key points

Strategy is a comprehensive plan for accomplishing an organisation's mission. *Strategic management* is a comprehensive and ongoing process aimed at formulating and implementing effective strategies. Many large organisations have corporate-level, business-level and functional-level strategies.

A corporate-level strategy is a plan used by an organisation to manage its operations across several businesses. A business-level strategy is the plan an organisation uses to conduct business in a particular industry. Porter suggests that organisations may formulate a differentiation strategy, a cost-leadership strategy or a focus strategy at the business level. Miles and Snow suggest that, at the business level, organisations may choose from a defender strategy, a prospector strategy, an analyser strategy or a reactor strategy. A functional-level strategy is the plan an organisation uses to manage its major operating departments in order to support corporate- and business-level strategies.

An organisation may decide to operate in a number of different, unrelated businesses. Organisations manage various businesses through *portfolio management techniques*:

- The BCG matrix classifies an organisation's various businesses as 'dogs, cash cows, question marks, or stars', according to market share and market growth rate.
- The GE Business Screen classifies businesses as 'winners, losers, question marks, average businesses or profit producers' according to industry attractiveness and competitive position.

A further aspect of strategic management is concerned with the matching of internal and external demands for human resources, and with integrating the management of human resources in overall organisational planning. Effective human resource management is of vital strategic importance to an organisation and contributes to an organisation's competitive advantage over competitors.

Important terms and concepts

analyser strategy (p.136)
BCG matrix (p.137)
business-level strategy (p.135)
competitive advantage (p.140)
competitive position (p.139)
corporate-level strategy (p.134)
defender strategy (p.136)
distinctive competence (p.132)
emergent strategy (p.133)
environmental analysis (p.132)
functional-level strategy (p.136)
GE Business Screen (p.138)
grand strategy alternatives (p.134)
growth strategy (p.135)
industry attractiveness (p.139)
intended strategy (p.133)
Miles and Snow's business stratety (p.135)

operational management (p.131)
organisational direction (p.131)
organisational opportunities (p.132)
organisational strengths (p.132)
organisational threats (p.132)
organisational weaknesses (p.132)
portfolio management techniques (p.136)
prospector strategy (p.136)
reactor strategy (p.136)
realised strategy (p.133)
retrenchment strategy (p.135)
stability strategy (p.135)
strategic business unit (p.134)
strategic HRM (p.140)
strategic management (p.130)
strategic management process (p.131)
strategy defined (p.130)
strategy evaluation (p.133)
strategy formulation (p.133)
strategy implementation (p.133)
SWOT analysis (p.132)
vertical integration (p.140)

Questions for review

1. Outline the steps involved in the strategic management process.

2. Differentiate between corporate, business and functional levels of strategy.

3. Evaluate the contribution portfolio models can make to strategic planning in an organisation.

4. Explain how employees can contribute to organisations in order to achieve a competitive advantage over competitors.

5. Write brief notes on:
   a. Strategic management
   b. Miles and Snow's business strategies
   c. Strategic human resource management.

10
CURRENT MANAGEMENT ISSUES

Objectives

This chapter will help you to:

- understand the implications of ethics and corporate social responsibility for organisations
- recognise the difficulties of managing through a recession
- identify the challenges of managing Generations X and Y
- recognise the increasing importance of talent management in organisations
- outline the advantages and disadvantages of virtual teams
- recognise a learning organisation
- understand the influence of knowledge workers in organisations
- recognise the contribution of diversity in the workplace
- explain employee engagement
- identify the relationship between flexible working and work–life balance.

10.1 Introduction

While management ideas and techniques come into and go out of fashion, interest in management theory and practice has increased in recent years as new issues and challenges have emerged. From a very wide range of issues which could be examined under the topic of current management issues, this chapter includes the following important challenges facing managers in the twenty-first century:

- ethics and corporate social responsibility
- managing through a recession
- managing Generations X and Y
- talent management
- managing virtual teams
- the learning organisation
- knowledge workers
- workplace diversity
- employee engagement
- flexible working and work–life balance.

10.2 Ethics and corporate social responsibility

The study of business ethics is not a new concept. Since the nineteenth century the need for ethical principles have been highlighted by social reformers. Current management literature on business ethics, along with the topic of ethics in general, is a growing field of research. As recently as a decade ago, many organisations viewed business ethics only in terms of administrative compliance with legal standards and adherence to internal rules and regulations. Today, the situation is different as attention to business ethics is on the rise across the world and many organisations realise that, in order to succeed, they must earn the respect and confidence of their customers. Organisations are now being asked and encouraged to improve their business practices in order to publically emphasise their legal and ethical compliance. Companies, professional firms and individuals are being held increasingly accountable for their actions, as demand grows for higher standards of corporate social responsibility. The study of ethics centres on choices facing individuals and **managerial ethics** has been defined as the standards of behaviour that guide individual managers in their work (Donaldson and Dunfee 1994). Managerial ethics, therefore, is concerned with:

- norms
- values
- rights and responsibilities
- fairness
- being part of an organisation that establishes and maintains a set of moral rules.

Every organisation operates an ethical code based on codes of conduct embedded in company culture and through the actions and decisions of senior management. One important area of managerial ethics is the way in which an organisation treats its employees. This includes working conditions, wages, hiring and firing, and employee privacy and respect. An organisation's ethical code will be influenced by the societal norms, values and culture in which it operates. Ethics may be viewed as a subset of culture and where cultural differences exist, for example, between different countries, different ethical standards are likely to prevail.

Another important area of managerial ethics is how employees treat the organisation. Examples of ethical issues for individual employees include:

- honesty
- confidentiality
- the divulging of organisational secrets (for example, by employees in electronics or computer software industries who may be tempted to sell future organisational plans to competitors).

Johns (1995) listed examples of unethical behaviour, which applies not only to managerial staff but is also evident in the actions of non-managerial staff. These include:

- giving gifts or gratuities to buyers in the hope of influencing them
- dishonesty towards customers and clients
- theft of employer's property and materials
- reading other people's mail for personal advantage.

The computer and the World Wide Web are two of the most significant inventions of the twentieth century. There are many ethical issues arising from this technology. It is now much easier to gain access to information and this can lead to data mining, workplace monitoring and privacy invasion.

Top management has the responsibility for enhancing ethical behaviour as it establishes an organisation's culture and defines what will and will not be acceptable behaviour (Griffin 2008).

Managing corporate social responsibility and ethics

The central question in the **corporate social responsibility** debate asks if the organisation exists solely to maximise the profits which it returns to its owners or, instead, if organisations and managers have a broader responsibility to society at large. Any philosophy or course of action that runs counter to public interest is not tolerated by society today (Hartley 1993). Organisations now face more critical scrutiny from stakeholders and operate in settings that are subject to an increasing number of regulations. As organisations, of necessity, interact with the environment in which they operate, they are regarded as having social responsibilities to society.

Corporate social responsibility has been defined by the European Commission as:

> A concept whereby companies integrate social and environmental concerns in their business operations and in their interaction with their stakeholders on a voluntary basis (http://ec.europa.eu).

Corporate social responsibility is part of the Europe 2020 strategy for smart, sustainable and inclusive growth. It can help to shape the kind of competitiveness model that Europe wants. Corporate social responsibility is more relevant than ever in the context of current economic crises. It can help to build (and rebuild) trust in business, which is vital for the health of Europe's social market economy. Organisations have many areas of corporate social responsibility, including:

- the natural environment
- product responsibility

- promotional activities
- organisational stakeholders.

The natural environment

Social responsibility towards the natural environment has grown substantially during the past three decades. Protection of the natural environment is now a crucial worldwide issue facing organisations and the public. As a result of many accidents and growing environmental damage caused by organisations, there are increasing demands from customers for organisations to operate more ethically in this area. Organisations have largely been blamed for damaging the quality of natural environments. Today's 'green' movement draws attention to some negative aspects of industry:

- the disposal of chemical and nuclear wastes
- the dangerous mercury levels in oceans
- the quantity of chemical pollutants in soil and in the food supply
- the littering of the environment with non-biodegradable plastics and other packaging materials.

Product responsibility

Manufacturing organisations are responsible for product safety. In many countries, consumer protection groups or associations test products for safety and report hazards found in products, such as electrical dangers in appliances, and other risks of injury. The testing and reporting activities of these organisations have encouraged organisations to eliminate product hazards. Organisations now accept that the products they generate are still their responsibility after their products have been sold to customers. Forward-thinking organisations also try to ensure that their products are used correctly and encourage their eventual disposal in an environmentally friendly way.

Promotional activities

While promotional activities of an organisation's products are designed to increase sales, there is often a temptation when promoting a product to exaggerate a product's attributes. Conscientious marketers face moral dilemmas when trying to make a service or product attractive while at the same time not misleading customers. This can be helped where organisations develop corporate marketing-ethics policies which provide guidelines for everyone in an organisation to follow. These policies should cover advertising standards, customer service, pricing, product development, distributor relations and general ethical standards.

Organisational stakeholders

All organisations have a variety of stakeholders. These are people who are directly affected by the practices of an organisation and who have a stake in its performance. Major stakeholders include:

- customers
- employees
- investors.

Organisations that practise social responsibility to customers attempt to treat customers fairly and honestly by charging fair prices, meeting delivery commitments, ensuring quality, and honouring guarantees and warranties.

Organisations that are socially responsible to employees maintain fair and reasonable standards in their treatment of individual employees, offer equal opportunities and place greater trust in relationships between individuals and groups. Such organisations also place an important emphasis on recruiting and training employees and on providing equal opportunities for ethnic minority groups and disabled people. Attitudinal barriers, however, provide the most serious obstacles to improving ethics in organisations and, where there is a need to change attitudes by improving the culture of an organisation, a strong commitment to improved ethics from top management must pervade an organisation (Donaldson 1989).

Some managers believe that organisations generally should promote the welfare of society — in addition to treating employees responsibly, taking care of the natural environment and having the best interests of organisational stakeholders to the fore. Examples of this include making contributions to charities, supporting not-for-profit foundations, taking a role in improving public health and providing education scholarships.

10.3 Managing through a recession

In a recession, setting goals and objectives is even more critical than during times of growth, because goals are likely to change more quickly in a recession. During recessionary times, in particular, all managers are focused on saving money for their organisations. Reducing costs throughout an organisation directly improves or protects profitability especially when sales are declining, and assists an organisation in maintaining staff levels during a recession. Making people redundant and recruiting again when the market recovers is expensive; therefore, human resource managers will be expected to bring innovative ideas and solutions leading to stronger organisations when recovery occurs.

One of the most important functions of management during a recession is to maintain communication with employees. Managers need to tell employees what the plan for the year is and what employees need to do to make it successful. The plan should address issues such as:

- how new sales can be generated
- where new customers can be found
- where savings can be made
- if production can do things faster, better and more reliably
- if raw materials can be purchased more cheaply.

Managers also need to focus on upskilling and re-skilling employees and should endeavour to make the best possible use of training budgets. Expectations of employees need to be managed. Creative, non-financial ways of motivating employees, such as recognition schemes, team-building days and employee awards, should be used. The impact of a recession causes employees to suffer additional stress, therefore, workplace support and occupational health provision need to be in place. Additionally, managers need to recognise the potential negative impact of 'survivor syndrome', if an organisation has made redundancies. Employees remaining in an organisation where there have been job cuts often suffer from guilt while coping with increased workloads.

If redundancies are inevitable, managers need to take advantage of natural wastage and offer voluntary redundancy terms, as enforced redundancies can have a serious negative impact on morale and performance. Redundancies need to be managed in a fair and equitable manner and employees should be informed about redundancy policies and procedures. Human resource managers should be equipped to deal with redundancy situations at both collective and individual levels, and should have a thorough understanding of laws relating to redundancy. Employees facing redundancy will need professional support and advice on how to cope, and redundant employees will also need some help in finding new employment. The treatment of employees who leave an organisation will impact on the attitudes and loyalty of those who remain.

10.4 Managing Generations X and Y

The workplace of the twenty-first century is rapidly changing, reflecting the widespread speed of change in the world generally. One of the newest diversity issues in the workplace is age diversity. Organisations now have a generational mix of people. Generational differences can affect recruitment, team building, dealing with change, motivation, and maintaining and increasing productivity. Generational employees are not new in the working world, but the generational gaps do pose interesting challenges for leadership and management in many organisations. Each generation is also motivated by different forces, and have come from different social upbringings.

Many human resource managers report conflicts between younger and older workers, reflecting each generation's very different values, skills, attitudes toward work and authority, and ways of operating. The differing age generations also create a communication gap. This communication gap is greater because of the different modes of communication each generation is used to. Research indicates that people's modes of communication are strongly influenced by their generational backgrounds. Each generation has distinct attitudes, behaviours, expectations, habits and motivations. Older employees are used to communicating face-to-face or by telephone. Younger employees prefer to communicate online. Learning how to communicate with different generations can greatly reduce the number of confrontations and misunderstandings in the workplace and the world of business.

Generation X, commonly abbreviated to **Gen X**, is the generation born between 1965 and 1980. Generation X came of age in an era of two-income families, when women were joining the workforce in large numbers. As a result, Generation X tends to be independent, resourceful and self-sufficient. In the workplace, Generation X values freedom and responsibility. Many in this generation display a casual disdain for authority and structured work hours. They dislike being micro-managed as they embrace a hands-off management philosophy. Generation X is less committed to one employer and more willing to change jobs to get ahead than previous generations. They adapt well to change and are tolerant of alternative lifestyles. Generation X is ambitious and eager to learn new skills but want to accomplish things on their own terms.

The Generation X mentality reflects a shift from a manufacturing economy to a service economy. They are the first generation to grow up with computers, and consequently are early adopters of social technology in the workplace. Core values of Generation X include:

- global thinking
- work–life balance
- techno-literacy
- diversity
- informality
- fun
- self-reliance
- pragmatism.

There are many differences between the traditional and new generation workplace. Employees from Generation X tend to favour the characteristics of the latter:

Traditional workplace	*New generation workplace*
Security from the institution	Security from within the individual
Promotions based on longevity	Promotions based on performance
Loyalty to the organisation	Loyalty to the team
Wait to be told what to do	Challenge authority
Respect based on position/title	Respect must be earned

Table 10.1 Traditional workplace versus new generation workplace

Generation X employees tend to be less motivated by promises of overtime pay and more motivated by personal satisfaction with their jobs. They want to learn new skills and have career development opportunities. They will change jobs more often than previous generations as they seek jobs that offer them better benefits and more opportunities for professional growth as well as for personal fulfilment. Generation X employees want, and expect, their employers to hear what they have to say. They want to understand the 'big picture' for the organisation and how this influences their employment and growth.

Generation Y, commonly abbreviated to **Gen Y**, is the generation born from 1981 onwards and is the newest generation in the workforce. One of the clear defining characteristics of this generation is technology. Generation Y was raised with the Internet and consequently rely on technology to perform their jobs better. Generation Y are known for their flexibility, and are more comfortable with diversity than other generations have been. The core values of Generation Y include:

- optimism
- civic duty
- confidence
- achievement
- sociability
- morality
- diversity.

Organisational leaders need to manage the expectations of Generation Y, and provide guidance and mentoring where necessary, in order to ensure that this generation can progress successfully in the workplace. Responding to generational differences and conflicts requires the same skills needed to deal with other diversity issues: awareness, communication and the ability to manage conflict. Awareness of the differences between the generations can help all employees to work more productively with each other. Knowing in advance how each generation can be triggered, either positively or negatively, can help organisations to develop balanced policies and can help individual managers and employees to structure their work interactions in ways that benefit all types of workers.

Effective communication strategies enable employees and managers to avoid low morale and lost productivity which normally accompanies the use of negative stereotypes. Communication skills are also essential for effective conflict resolution skills. Developing employees' awareness of inter-generational issues and enhancing their skills in conflict resolution and communication should contribute to increased effectiveness in the workplace.

10.5 Talent management

Talent management is a process that emerged in the 1990s and continues to be adopted, as more companies come to realise that employee talents and skills drive their business success. **Talent management** refers to the process of attracting highly skilled people to work for a company, developing and integrating new workers, developing and retaining current workers, and succession planning. The process of attracting and retaining profitable employees has become increasingly more competitive between organisations and is referred to as 'the war for talent'. Talent management has been defined by the Chartered Institute of Personnel and Development as:

> The systematic attraction, identification, development, engagement/retention and deployment of those individuals who are of particular value to an organisation, either in view of their 'high potential' for the future or because they are fulfilling business/operation-critical roles (www.cipd.co.uk).

This definition underlines the importance of recognising that it is not enough to just attract individuals with high potential. Developing, managing and retaining those individuals as part of a planned strategy for talent is equally important, as is adopting systems to measure the return on this investment. More organisations are also now broadening their definitions, looking at the talents of all their staff and working on ways to develop staff strengths.

Talent management brings together a number of important human resources and management initiatives. Organisations that formally decide to manage their talent undertake a strategic analysis of their current human resource management processes. This is to ensure that a co-ordinated, performance-oriented approach is adopted. Organisations adopting a talent management approach will focus on co-ordinating and integrating:

- recruitment — ensuring the right people are attracted to the organisation
- retention — developing and implementing practices that reward and support employees
- employee development — ensuring continuous informal and formal learning and development
- leadership development — specific development programmes for existing and future leaders
- performance management — specific processes that nurture and support performance, including feedback/measurement
- workforce planning — planning for business and general changes, including the older workforce and current/future skills shortages
- culture — development of a positive, progressive and high performance way of operating.

A proactive, strategic approach to talent management offers considerable organisational benefits in terms of developing a pool of talent as a resource to meet identified needs. Talent management must be supported by senior management, but line managers also need to be engaged from an early stage to ensure that they are committed to organisational approaches for developing and managing talent. Talent management is a dynamic process that has to be frequently reviewed to ensure that organisational requirements are still being met in the light of changing business priorities. Ultimately, organisational success is the most effective evaluation of talent management.

10.6 Managing virtual teams

A **virtual team** is a group of individuals who work across time, space and organisational boundaries with links strengthened by webs of communication technology. Members of virtual teams communicate electronically, so they may seldom or never meet face-to-face. Virtual teams are made possible by a proliferation of fibre optic technology that has significantly increased the scope of off-site communication. Virtual teams allow companies to procure the best talent without geographical restrictions.

Virtual teams are essentially governed by the same fundamental principles as traditional teams, except for one critical difference. This difference is the way the team members communicate. Instead of using the full spectrum and dynamics of in-office face-to-face exchange, they now rely on special communication channels enabled by modern technologies, such as e-mails, faxes, phone calls and teleconferences, and virtual meetings.

Due to more limited face-to-face communication opportunities, the success and effectiveness of a virtual team is more dependent on how the team is managed than in the case of traditional teams. Managers of virtual teams need to pay more attention to maintaining clear goals, performance standards and communication rules. Team members should make greater efforts to communicate clearly, unambiguously, constructively and positively through channels of technology because of limitations on non-verbal communication such as the lack of face-to-face and other body-language cues. Communication problems may also be magnified by disparity among technology infrastructures, as well as differences in technology proficiency among team members.

Cultural differences among team members may also lead to instances of miscommunication since different cultures tend to contain certain biases, assumptions or different views of the world. Kayworth and Leidner (2000) summarise that, regardless of the source, the 'cultural factor' may lead to information distortion and instances of miscommunication. Communication among global virtual teams may be extremely difficult to manage and less effective than in more traditional settings. People have varying assumptions about what to expect from each other. To avoid a build-up of misunderstandings in a virtual organisation it is critical to replace implicit assumptions with clear rules and protocols that everyone understands and agrees upon, especially for communication.

Not everyone can perform well in a virtual team environment. Team members should be self-motivated and able to work independently. They need to be able to keep working effectively without much external control or structure. Team members also need to be results-oriented. Unless the person shows clear results, there is nobody around to see how intense his or her work activities are.

One of the biggest challenges of managing virtual teams is building and maintaining trust between the team members. Trust is critical for unblocking communication between members and for sustaining motivation of each person involved. The issue of trust needs special attention at any stage of team existence. Distance also brings other issues, such as team members having to negotiate multiple time zones and requiring them to reorganise their workdays to accommodate the schedules of each other. Team managers must be comfortable with relinquishing traditional control over employees, while remaining committed to mentoring and evaluating them. Overall, virtual team managers must pay particular attention to the challenges posed by the physical separation between members.

10.7 The learning organisation

The learning organisation has been the subject of much interest in management literature recently. Organisations that promote the learning concept attempt to integrate organisational improvement with ongoing and shared employee learning and development. The basic rationale for such organisations is that in situations of rapid change only those that are flexible, adaptive and productive will excel. For this to happen, it is argued, organisations need to 'discover how to tap people's commitment and capacity to learn at *all* levels' (Senge 1990). Pedler *et al.* (1996) define a learning organisation as:

> an organisation that facilitates the learning of all its members and continuously transforms itself

and give the principal characteristics of a learning organisation as:

- the creation of opportunities for learning, not just in a formal sense but also from everyday actions which are debated, reviewed and questioned
- the design of structures and cultures that ensure all employees feel that they are encouraged to learn, to question existing rules and practices, to experiment with new ideas and are empowered to contribute to decisions at all levels
- the development of managers who are totally committed to facilitating learning by the adoption of open and participative approaches to decision-making
- the acceptance that mistakes will be made, but that they are an essential part of the learning process
- the provision of learning opportunities for all employees, not just managers, and the assumption that, with appropriate guidance, each employee should assume responsibility for his or her own learning and development
- the implementation of systems (accounting and other data) designed to be accessed by users rather than experts
- the breaking down of barriers between different individuals and departments to encourage open communication and ways of working.

The concept of the learning organisation views an organisation in its totality; that means looking for links between different management functions and departments and regarding continuous improvement as a never-ending process. A learning organisation, therefore, is one that works to facilitate the lifelong learning and personal development of all employees while continually transforming itself to respond to changing demands and needs.

A key feature of a learning organisation is that it is designed to overcome many of the obstacles that prevent learning and development. These obstacles can be formed by individuals or by organisations. Employee obstacles to learning may be formed by earlier educational experiences or they may lack the intellectual skills or learning styles to enable effective learning to be achieved. In the case of organisational obstacles, the organisation may display few signs of obvious commitment to learning or supervisors may make it known that they are not supportive of staff engaging in further learning and development.

In a learning organisation, the challenge for senior managers, therefore, is to encourage openness and to accept that errors and uncertainty are inevitable features of organisational life. The creation of a blame-free culture, where employees are able to admit mistakes and recognise that mistakes are part of the improvement process, is also an essential part of the learning organisation. The main benefits of a learning organisation are:

- maintaining levels of innovation and remaining competitive
- being better placed to respond to external pressures
- having the knowledge to better link resources to customer needs
- improving quality of outputs at all levels
- improving corporate image by becoming more people-oriented
- increasing the pace of change within the organisation.

Probst and Büchel (1997) believe that survival of organisations in an increasingly competitive environment will depend on its capacity for **organisational learning**, which must be ongoing. They suggest that communication and transparency are essential components of a learning organisation. Ghoshal and Bartlett (1998) argue that there has been a gradual fading of corporate management's quarter-century-long preoccupation with strategic planning. The rapid pace of change in organisational environments has undermined the relevance of long-range planning. This has forced managers to focus less on the task of forecasting and planning for the future and more on the challenge of being highly sensitive to emerging changes. These changes create organisations which are constantly experimenting with appropriate responses, so that they can quickly spread the information and knowledge gained for organisation-wide benefits. Thus, according to Ghoshal and Bartlett, the era of strategic planning is being replaced by an age of organisational learning.

10.8 Knowledge workers

The term **knowledge worker** was coined by Peter Drucker in the mid-1950s, for one who works primarily with information or one who develops and uses knowledge in the workplace. Knowledge workers are individuals who are involved in the creation of new information or new knowledge, as distinct from those individuals who are categorised as **data workers**. Data workers are individuals who use, manipulate, process and disseminate information. To qualify as knowledge workers, the workers need to *apply* their knowledge. As contemporary businesses have become more complex, the demand for expertise has increased and knowledge workers have replaced the more traditional labour force.

Drucker has frequently argued that improving knowledge worker productivity is the most important task of the twenty-first century. He suggested that the task is not to *manage* knowledge workers, but to *lead* them. Drucker also believed that *management* can actually make it more difficult for knowledge workers to attain goals, but *leadership* is essential to their success.

Nonaka (1991) advocated a view of knowledge as renewable and changing, and suggested that knowledge workers were the agents for that change. Nonaka also believed that knowledge-creating companies should be focused primarily on the task of innovation. This laid the foundation for the new practice of **knowledge management** which evolved in the 1990s to support knowledge workers with standard tools and processes. Knowledge management typically focuses on organisational objectives such as improved performance, competitive advantage, innovation, the sharing of lessons learned, integration and continuous improvement of the organisation.

Tapscott and Williams (2006) also see a strong and ongoing linkage between knowledge workers and innovation, but he thinks the pace and manner of interaction have become more advanced. He believes that social media tools now drive powerful forms of collaboration. Knowledge workers engage in peer-to-peer knowledge sharing across organisational and company boundaries, forming networks of expertise. Social networks are important for knowledge workers and they rely on their networks to understand their knowledge and to compare themselves and their abilities to others inside and outside their organisation.

The success of knowledge-intensive organisations depends on their ability to convert their human capital (the knowledge, skills and experience of their employees) into intellectual capital, i.e. the products and services that have value in the marketplace. An organisation's competitive advantage revolves around its most advanced talent — those leading-edge knowledge workers who solve challenging problems, develop new products and take the business in novel directions. In addition, knowledge work depends on a combination of technical skills, behavioural competencies and attitudes, which also adds to the complexity of motivating, measuring and managing performance. According to the Chartered Institute of Personnel and Development, knowledge workers have the following, specific characteristics:

- they need to apply highly structured technical knowledge to ambiguous client demands
- they work in an autonomous fashion within fluid leadership structures
- they are normally ambitious and upwardly mobile, and their key focus is the development of their own careers (www.cipd.co.uk).

Miller (2002) suggests that organisations wishing to attract knowledge workers need to align their business strategy with their corporate culture and to ensure that their workers are personally involved in the ownership of strategy and culture. Miller also points out the following attributes that differentiate an employer from a knowledge worker:

- vision — exciting, big and engaging ideas
- direction — a sense that their career is 'going somewhere'
- impact — the opportunity to make a difference
- challenge — going beyond current capabilities
- listening — knowing they will be heard
- validation — recognition and appreciation of their skills and contribution
- learning — acquiring new skills
- autonomy — the power to make decisions
- values — a fit between their own and organisational values.

Effective organisations allow knowledge workers to place themselves, according to their strengths, where they can make the greatest contributions. According to Drucker (2000), knowledge workers do not believe they are paid to work 9.00 a.m. to 5.00 p.m. Instead, they believe that they are paid to be effective, and organisations that understand this will be able to attract, motivate and retain the best performers. This, Drucker believes, will be the single biggest factor for competitive advantage in the early decades of this century.

10.9 Workplace diversity

Workforce diversity is an issue which poses numerous challenges for managers. Workplace diversity is now one of the main drivers of change in the Irish workplace. Over the past decade, large numbers of immigrants arrived in Ireland. Resulting from this, the population of Ireland is more ethnically diverse than at any previous time. Migrant workers are entitled to the same working rights as Irish nationals. Managing diversity is about ensuring that all employees have the opportunity to maximise their potential and enhance their self-development and their contribution to the organisation. It recognises that people from different backgrounds can bring fresh ideas and perceptions, which can improve the manner in which work is done, products are manufactured and services provided. Managing diversity successfully helps organisations to nurture creativity and innovation. The term 'diversity' is often used broadly to refer to many variables, including, but not limited to:

- race
- gender
- religion
- colour
- national origin
- disability
- sexual orientation
- age
- education
- geographic origin
- skill characteristics.

Diversity acknowledges that no one style of working is invariably the right one. It focuses on ensuring that an organisation is recruiting staff with the potential to help the company to meet its objectives and that the organisation is maximising the potential of all employees to meet those objectives. Diversity is, in effect, about good management.

Diversity differs from discrimination, because diversity is about variety and differences while discrimination concerns treating people differently through prejudice. Diversity goes beyond a list of descriptors because it is about creating a workplace environment that maximises the potential of every individual member of the workforce and appreciates that every employee is diverse — not just those 'on the list'.

Many organisations are finding that diversity can be a source of competitive advantage in the marketplace. Organisations that manage diversity effectively will become known among minorities as good places to work, and in turn these organisations will generally have lower levels of turnover and absenteeism. By discriminating on the basis of gender, race, ethnicity or disability, managers run the risk of neglecting or overlooking talented employees. The consequence is that the organisation fails to maximise its full human resource potential and valuable resources are wasted through underutilising the competence of existing employees or losing talented staff to other organisations.

10.10 Employee engagement

Engagement at work was conceptualised by William A. Kahn (1990) as the 'harnessing of organisational members' selves to their work roles'. Engagement is not about driving employees in order to work harder, but about providing the conditions under which they will work more effectively. Employee engagement can be seen as a combination of commitment to the organisation and to its values plus a willingness to help out colleagues (organisational citizenship). It goes beyond job satisfaction and is not simply motivation. Engagement is something the employee has to offer, it cannot be 'required' as part of the employment contract. Organisations are now realising that 'engaged' employees are more productive, more loyal, deliver higher levels of customer satisfaction and are more likely to lead to organisational success.

Engagement has three dimensions:

- *Emotional engagement* — being very involved emotionally with one's work.
- *Cognitive engagement* — focusing very hard while at work.
- *Physical engagement* — being willing to 'go the extra mile' for an employer.

Research conducted by the Chartered Institute for Personnel and Development into employee attitudes found that the main drivers of employee engagement were:

- having opportunities to feed views upwards
- feeling well-informed about what is happening in the organisation
- believing that one's manager is committed to the organisation (www.cipd.co.uk).

Similarly, research by Robinson *et al.* (2004) concluded that the main driver of engagement is a sense of feeling valued and involved. This includes:

- involvement in decision-making
- freedom to voice ideas, to which managers listen
- feeling enabled to perform well
- having opportunities to develop the job
- feeling the organisation is concerned for employees' health and well-being.

Engagement levels are influenced by employees' personal characteristics, and a minority of employees are likely to resist becoming engaged in their work. Employees are also influenced by the jobs they do and the experiences they have at work. The way in which both senior management and line managers behave towards, and communicate with, employees, plus the way in which work is organised and jobs defined, contributes significantly towards making work meaningful and engaging.

Adopting an effective engagement strategy can provide an opportunity for employees to acquire new skills and to work alongside professionals in other parts of the business. The development of a robust employer 'brand' can also support positive employee engagement. Engaged employees are more likely than disengaged employees to act as organisational advocates and can play a powerful role in promoting their organisation as an employer of choice.

10.11 Flexible working and work–life balance

Prior to the current recession in Ireland, a period of rapid economic growth was accompanied by a strong surge in the number of women in employment. This led to a significant increase in the proportion of dual-earner families. These changes have brought the issue of balancing work and family commitments to the fore. Flexible working arrangements in companies have been identified as an important means of balancing work and personal commitments. Flexibility in the workplace is important for attracting talent, retaining valuable employees, raising morale and job satisfaction, improving productivity, and reducing stress and burnout.

Flexibility in working time includes a variety of arrangements for part-time work, job-sharing, flexi-time, fixed-term contracts, subcontracting and career/employment-break schemes. Flexible working is the basis of work–life balance. Organisations also have a statutory obligation to provide certain family-friendly initiatives such as maternity leave and parental leave. Placing most of the emphasis on employees who have to care for young children, however, is too narrow a focus and can alienate some employees as it is not only children who are dependent on others. In Ireland, many people already act as carers for elderly or disabled members of their family. Work–life balance, therefore, is not just for women. Many men stand to benefit in their roles as fathers, partners or dependants. Society also benefits, since stronger and more stable families provide good adult role models, fewer broken relationships, and a reduction in crime and other anti-social behaviour.

According to the Chartered Institute of Personnel and Development, there are benefits to business when introducing policies to support work–life balance issues. These include:

- higher productivity and competitiveness
- increased flexibility and customer service, for example to cover for absence and holidays
- raised morale, motivation, commitment and engagement

- reduced absenteeism
- improved recruitment and retention of a diverse workforce
- wanting to become an 'employer of choice'
- meeting legal requirements (www.cipd.co.uk).

In an Irish context, a national framework for family-friendly policies was established under the Programme for Prosperity and Fairness, to focus on facilitating and supporting the development of family-friendly policies at the enterprise level. Subsequently, the National Framework Committee on Family Friendly Policies was established to promote and raise awareness of family-friendly working practices with the promotion of annual family-friendly days. The focus has now shifted to the promotion of work–life balance days in an effort to include employees who do not have families.

Having an organisational policy on flexible working is a positive step towards providing employees with a positive work–life balance. From a human resource manager perspective, understanding the relationship between flexible working arrangements and career development is important to the development of career management systems which are inclusive of employees who chose to reduce their working hours. The success, or otherwise, of flexible working arrangements is dependent on several factors, including line-manager predisposition to the notion of flexible working and the prevailing culture within the organisation, as well as the dispersion of power.

In conclusion, flexible working presents opportunities to employees to continue their professional lives while tending to their family responsibilities, and is an important aspect of work–life balance policies. They play an important part particularly in the facilitation of female labour-market participation.

10.12 Key points

This chapter focuses on ten current management issues.

Ethics involves personal beliefs about what constitutes right and wrong behaviour. The ethical context of an organisation is founded on the shared values of its individual managers and on the dominant messages arising from organisational practices. Corporate social responsibility is the set of obligations an organisation has in order to protect and enhance the society in which it functions.

Managing through a recession requires human resource managers, in particular, to provide leadership in their organisations. Human resource managers should communicate frequently, openly and honestly with all employees regarding future plans for the organisation. Managers need to provide methods of up-skilling, re-skilling, motivating and rewarding employees who are to remain in employment, and also need to provide guidance and career advice for employees due to become redundant as a result of the recession.

Managing Generations X and Y requires managers to overlook stereotypes and to pay attention to individual needs and motivations of all employees. Generations X and Y have entered the workplace of the twenty-first century where working practices and managerial and organisational expectations are changing rapidly. Previous generations entered the workplace with set working patterns and managerial hierarchies firmly in place. For the first time in history, four generations of employees are now working together. Each group has its unique strengths and differences, and is often misunderstood by the others, thus frequently resulting in conflict.

Talent management seeks to focus on the potential of its employees. As the recruitment and selection process is very expensive, it is important to place employees in positions where their skills are being utilised extensively. Many managers put considerable effort in attracting employees to their organisations but spend little time in retaining and developing talent. In the current economic climate, many organisations have had to re-evaluate the contribution of their employees; therefore, this should provide a good opportunity for executing a talent management system as a means of optimising the performance of each employee and the organisation.

Managing virtual teams, in comparison to managing traditional teams, poses additional management challenges because of limited communication channels, cultural differences between team members, working in different time zones, and less face-to-face control and structure. Managers also need to ensure that team members are self-motivated and are capable of working independently.

The principal characteristics of a *learning organisation* include a commitment to continual improvement for the benefit both of the individuals within the organisation and the organisation as a whole, and communication systems and attitudes that create an open and blame-free organisational culture in which lifelong learning can take place. Managers have a crucial part to play in the development, ongoing maintenance and success of the learning organisation.

Knowledge workers are people employed because of their knowledge of a subject matter, rather than their ability to perform manual labour. They produce and distribute ideas and information rather than goods or services. They are individuals with different aspirations from the hierarchy-conscious employees of previous generations; they are also mobile and are willing to leave organisations. Hiring knowledge workers is difficult, but retaining them is even more difficult. They perform best when empowered to take responsibility for their actions and are given opportunities to do things their own way. Knowledge workers should be treated as an asset rather than a cost.

The workforce in organisations today is becoming increasingly diverse, a development that affects employees' lives and poses numerous challenges to managers. Managers need to create diversity awareness and to appreciate the numerous positive benefits of a diverse workforce.

Employee engagement is becoming increasingly important for organisations that want to remain competitive. Engaged employees have a positive impact on productivity and on the financial performance of organisations, have less absenteeism, and provide better customer service in comparison to their disengaged counterparts. Engaged employees also speak enthusiastically about the organisation to colleagues, potential employees and customers. Employee engagement suggests that employees are motivated by intrinsic factors such as personal growth and working to a common purpose such as being part of a larger organisation, rather than simply focusing on extrinsic factors such as pay or rewards.

Flexible working and work–life balance are now part of modern-day organisations, particularly with the increased participation of women in the labour force. The benefits of flexible working arrangements contribute to a better balance between work and home for both male and female employees.

Important terms and concepts

employee engagement (p.160)
ethics and corporate social responsibility (p.145)
flexible working and work–life balance (p.161)
Generation X (p.150)
Generation Y (p.151)
knowledge workers (p.156)
learning organisation (p.155)
managerial ethics (p.145)
managing Generations X and Y (p.149)
managing virtual teams (p.153)
natural environment (p.147)
organisational learning (p.156)
organisational stakeholders (p.148)
product responsibility (p.147)
promotional activities (p.147)
talent management (p.152)
workplace diversity (p.158)

Questions for review

1. Examine the implications of ethics and corporate social responsibility in the management of contemporary organisations.

2. Examine the function of the human resource manager in managing through recessionary times.

3. Identify some of the barriers faced by Generations X and Y in organisations and suggest how these barriers may be overcome.

4. Discuss some advantages and disadvantages for employees when working as part of a virtual team.

5. Explain how organisational learning takes place, illustrating the advantages for employees when employed in a learning organisation.

6. Discuss current management issues relevant to managers in Irish organisations.

7. Discuss the contribution of knowledge workers to organisations.

8. Outline the advantages of having a diverse workforce.

9. Discuss how employee engagement can be used to motivate employees.

10. Explain how flexible working can contribute to work–life balance.

REFERENCES

ACAS (Advisory Conciliation and Arbitration Service). 1982. *Workplace Communications*, Advisory Booklet no. 8. London: ACAS.

Aktouf, O. 1996. *Traditional Management and Beyond*. Montreal: Morin.

Alderfer, P. 1969. 'An Empirical Test of a New Theory of Human Needs', *Organisational Behaviour and Human Performance*, 4, 142–75

Armstrong, M. and A. Baron. 2004. *Managing Performance: Performance Management in Action*. London: Chartered Institute of Personnel and Development.

Barney, J. 1996. 'Strategic factor markets', *Management Science*, December, 1231–41.

Beer, M., B. Spector and P.R. Lawrence. 1984. *Managing Human Assets*. New York: Free Press.

Berridge, J. and C. Cooper. 1994. 'The Employee Assistance Programme: Its Role in Organisational Coping and Excellence', *Personnel Review*, 23(7), 4–20.

Bratton, J. and J. Gold. 2003. *Human Resource Management: Theory and Practice* (3rd edition). London: Macmillan.

Capowski. 1994. 'Anatomy of The Leader: Where Are The Leaders of Tomorrow?' *Management Review*, March, 12.

Daft, R. 1998. *Organisation Theory and Design* (6th edition). Cincinnati, Ohio: South-Western.

Donaldson,T. 1989. *Key Issues in Business Ethics*. San Diego: Academic Press.

Donaldson, T. and T.W. Dunfee. 1994. 'Toward a Unified Conception of Business Ethics: An Integrative Social Contracts Theory', *Academy of Management Review* 19(2), 252–84.

Drucker, P. 1954. *The Practice of Management*, London: Heinemann.

Drucker, P. 2000. 'Managing knowledge means managing oneself', *Leader to Leader*, 16, 1–5.

Eisenhardt, K.M., J.L. Kaahwajy and L.J. Bourgeois. 1997. 'How Management Teams Can Have a Good Fight', *Harvard Business Review*, July–August, 77–89.

Fayol, H. 1916. *Administration Industrielle et Générale* (1916), translated as *General and Industrial Management*. London: Pitman 1949.

Ghoshal, S. and C.A. Bartlett. 1998. *The Individualised Corporation: A Fundamentally New Approach to Management*. London: Heinemann.

Griffin, R.W. 2008. *Management* (9th edition). New York: Houghton Mifflin.

Guest, D.E. 1987. 'Human Resource Management and Industrial Relations', *Journal of Management Studies*, 24(5), 503–21.

Guest, D., J. Storey and W. Tate. 1997. *Innovation: Opportunity through People. Consultative Document*. London: Institute of Personnel and Development. June.

Hannagan, T. 2008. *Management: Concepts & Practices* (5th edition). London: Financial Times Management.

Harrison, R. 2000. *Employee Development* (2nd edition). London: Institute of Personnel Management.

Hartley, R.F. 1993. *Business Ethics: Violations of the Public Trust*. New York: John Wiley.

Herriot, P. and C. Pemberton. 1997. Facilitating New Deals. *Human Resource Management Journal*, 7(1), 45–56.

Hofer, C. and D. Schendel, 1978. *Strategy Formulation: Analytical Concepts*. Ohio: West Publishing.

Johns, T. 1995. 'Don't Be Afraid of The Moral Maze', *People Management*, October, 32–4.

Kahn, W. A. 1990. 'Psychological conditions of personal engagement and disengagement at work', *The Academy of Management Journal*, 33 (4), 692–724.

Kayworth, T. and D. Leidner. 2000. 'The global virtual manager: A prescription for success', *European Management Journal*, 18 (2), 183–194.

Kotter, J. 1986. *The General Managers*. New York: Free Press.

Kotter, J. 1990. *A Force for Change: How Leadership differs from Management*. New York: Free Press.

Lawrence P.R. and J.W. Lorsch. 1967. *Organisation and Environment*. Boston: Harvard University Press.

Legge, K. 1995. 'Human Resource Management: Rhetoric, Reality and Hidden Agendas' in *Human Resource Management, a critical text*, J. Storey (ed.). London: Routledge.

Lewin, K., R. Lippit and R.K. White. 1939. 'Patterns of aggressive behavior in experimentally created social climates', *Journal of Social Psychology*, 10, 271–301.

Marchington, M. and A. Wilkinson. 2000. *Core Personnel and Development* (2nd edition). London: Institute of Personnel and Development.

Miles, R.E. and C.C. Snow. 1978. *Organisational Strategy, Structure and Process*. New York: McGraw-Hill.

Miller, R. 2002. 'Motivating and managing knowledge workers: Blending strategy and culture in knowledge organizations', *Knowledge Management Review* 5(1), 6–19.

Mintzberg, H. 1973. *The Nature of Managerial Work*. New York: Harper & Row.

Mintzberg, H. 1979. *The Structuring of Organisations — A Synthesis of the Research*. New Jersey: Prentice Hall.

Mullins, L.J. 2007. *Management and Organizational Behaviour* (8th edition). London: Financial Times Pitman Publishing.

Naylor, J. 2004. *Management* (2nd edition). London: Financial Times Pitman Publishing.

Needles, E., H.R. Anderson and J.C. Caldwell. 1999. *Principles of Accounting*. Boston: Houghton Mifflin.

Nonaka, I. 1991. 'The Knowledge Creating Company', *Harvard Business Review*, 69, November–December, 96–104.

Northouse, P.G. 2007. *Leadership Theory & Practice* (4th edition). Thousand Oaks, CA: Sage.

Pearce, J.A. and F. David. 1987. 'Corporate Mission Statements: The Bottom Line', *Academy of Management Executive*, May 1987, 109.

Pedler, M., J. Burgoyne and T. Boydell. 1996. *The Learning Company: A Strategy for Sustainable Development*. London: McGraw-Hill.

Peters, T.J. and R.H. Waterman. 1989. *In Search of Excellence: Lessons from America's Best-run Companies*. London: Harper & Row.

Porter, M. 1980. *Competitive Strategy: Techniques for Analyzing Industries and Competitors*. New York: Free Press.

Porter, M. 1996. 'Competitive Strategy: Techniques for Analyzing Industries and Competitors', *Academy of Management Journal*, April, 255–91.

Probst, G.J.B. and B.S.T. Büchel. 1997. *Organisational Learning: The Competitive Advantage of the Future*. London: Prentice Hall.

Quinn, F. 2002. *Crowning the Customer: How to Become Customer Driven*. Dublin: O'Brien Press.

Robinson, D., S. Perryman and S. Hayday. 2004. *The Drivers of Employee Engagement*. Brighton: Institute for Employment Studies.

Senge, P.M. 1990. *The Fifth Discipline: The Art and Practice of the Learning Organisation*. New York: Doubleday.

Steers, R.M. and L.W. Porter. (eds), 1991. *Motivation and Work Behaviour* (5th edition). New York: McGraw-Hill.

Tapscott, D. and A. D. Williams. 2006. *How Mass Collaboration Changes Everything*. New York: Penguin.

Taylor, F.W. 1911. *Principles of Scientific Management*. New York: Harper & Brothers.

Wallace, J., P. Gunnigle and G. McMahon. 2004. *Industrial Relations in Ireland* (3rd edition). Dublin: Gill & Macmillan.